# HYPNOTHERAPY IN PRACTICE
A Practical Handbook for Health Care Professionals

### Edited by Samuel Abudarham

**Association of Hypnotherapists in Health Care**

*Published by the Association of Hypnotherapists in Health Care*
*199 Pershore Road, Birmingham B5 7PF*

*First Published 1991*
© *1991 Samuel Abudarham*

*British Library Cataloguing in Publication Data*
*Hypnotherapy in Practice*
    1. Hypnotherapy
    I. Abudarham, Samuel.   II.   Association of Hypnotherapists in health care
    615.8512

*ISBN    0  9517322  0  X*

*All rights reserved, including translation. No part of this publication may be reprinted or reproduced or transmitted in any form or by any means, electronic or mechanical, including photocopying, recording or duplication in any information storage and retrieval system, without permission in writing from the publishers.*

*Printed at Aston University in Birmingham,*
*Great Britain*

# Dedication

To the memory of my late mother LEA ABUDARHAM

# Contents

LIST OF CONTRIBUTORS — vii

PREFACE AND ACKNOWLEDGEMENTS — viii - x

PART I — THEORETICAL ISSUES

*Chapter 1*    The Phenomenon    S. Abudarham    13

PART II — THE PRACTICE AND CLINICAL IMPLICATIONS

*Chapter 2*    Patient Selection and Preparation    S. Abudarham    35

*Chapter 3*    Hypnosis - The Practice    S. Abudarham    48

*Chapter 4*    Hypnotherapy in the Management of Psychologically Related Problems    M. J. W. Hughes and S. Abudarham    77

*Chapter 5*    Hypnotherapy for Communication Disorders    S. Abudarham    97

*Chapter 6*    Use of Hypnosis for Physical and Related Conditions    F. Frazer    109

*Chapter 7*    Miscellaneous Conditions    S. Abudarham    125

BIBLIOGRAPHY — 138

INDEX — 144

APPENDICES

   A: 'Eye-Fixation' and 'Progressive Relaxation' Induction Routine    146

   B: Ideo-Motor (I.M.R.) Finger-Signalling Response Routine    147

   C: Ego-Strengthening Routine    148

# List of Contributors

**Samuel Abudarham,** MSc, LCST, MCST, DipCST
Principal Lecturer in Speech Pathology and Therapeutics,
Birmingham Polytechnic.
Chairman of Association for Hypnosis in Health Care

**Fred Frazer,** PhD, BA (Hons), MCSP
Director of Physical Rehabilitation Programme (Physiotherapist),
Selly Oak Hospital, Birmingham.
Vice Chairman of Association for Hypnosis in Health Care

**Malcolm J. W. Hughes,** PhD, BSc.
Senior Lecturer in Biomedical Sciences, Birmingham Polytechnic, and
 Psychologist.

# Preface

Having been, with my colleague Dr Hughes, a pioneer in the United Kingdom in providing formal training in Hypnotherapy to members of the Health Care Professions, it became clear to me that there was a lot of interest in its use in health care. For what was probably the first time in the U.K., a course had been made available and had been designed with the Health Care Professional, and the conditions they are confronted with in the course of their work, in mind. The most precocious turned out to be Speech Therapists and very soon after our first course, the College of Speech Therapists, after consultation with appropriate professionals and some of its members, acknowledged that hypnotherapy was a legitimate therapy for some individuals suffering communication disorders.

The range of participants in our courses evidenced the interest that many other professionals had in hypnotherapy. Some of them, however, belonged to professions which still seemed to be very nervous about its use and many are still so, to the extent that they have still not even discussed addressing the issues. Nonetheless, the grass root membership is leading the way and among those attending our courses have been physiotherapists, psychiatric nurses, occupational therapists, health visitors, psychotherapists, psychologists, dietitians and counsellors.

Soon after our first course, other organisations offered training in hypnosis but at a very basic level. It was clearly a time when several people had been considering the value of hypnosis as a therapeutic strategy. A somewhat reluctant and perhaps cautious acknowledgement in a study conducted by the British Medical Association that hypnosis could be beneficial in the treatment of conditions such as some types of voice disorders, stuttering and other conditions traditionally treated in other health care fields, and the recommendation by some eminent hypnotherapists in the medical profession that members of the paramedical (health care) professions who had received appropriate training could legitimately use hypnosis, encouraged many to seek formal training.

After seven years of providing such training, the needs of the health care professions became crystallised in our minds. Many who attended our courses had been practising self-taught hypnosis and sought a more formal training. It soon became clear to us that the available literature was more suitable for the medical, dental and psychological professions. There was, to our knowledge, no book which had been written with the Health Care Professional in mind. Many of the conditions discussed in the literature, to date, included those which required medical or clinical psychological training and those that did not were addressed assuming such training.

By responding to the declared needs of our trainees and taking heed of the feedback they gave us following our courses, we soon arrived at a programme content and teaching strategies which were tailor-made for the Health Care

Professionals and the conditions they traditionally treated. This book closely follows this tried and tested programme format.

The objective of the present project was to write a book which could serve as a training manual. As such, it was not designed to be over-burdened by academia but should be practically orientated. We recognised, however, that the credibility of a book is often reflected by its reference to the published literature, both theoretical and clinical/experimental. We thus devote Chapter 1 to addressing a lot of these theoretical issues and provide a fairly comprehensive review of the literature.

Whereas the rest of the chapters are more practically orientated, they nevertheless contain a modest number of references to the published literature but they largely reflect the authors' clinical insights and experience.

In Chapters 2 and 3 we address basic clinical issues. We have found that many inadequately trained hypnotherapists decide upon using hypnosis on prescriptive grounds and do not take enough care to consider the rationale for its use with the particular client. Similarly, they often do not take appropriate steps to prepare the client. This 'negligence' often results in a claim that 'hypnosis has not worked'! Chapter 2 discusses criteria for rationalising the appropriate use of hypnosis and the subsequent strategies for preparing the client.

Chapter 3 addresses the actual practice of hypnosis. It includes descriptions of several induction, hypnotherapy and hypnoanalytic techniques. These are illustrated by appropriate case studies. Throughout, the warning is emphasised that, particularly hypnoanalytic techniques must be employed with caution and certainly not by practitioners who do not have a sound knowledge of the nature and treatment of psychological problems.

The last three chapters address specific disorders which are treatable by hypnosis. The point is made that hypnosis is rarely effective on its own and that it serves its best purpose as an adjunct to any profession's traditional therapeutic strategies. Chapter 4 describes the use of hypnotherapy and hypnoanalysis for a variety of psychologically-related disorders. The conditions addressed are those most often met in health care work.

Chapter 5 addresses the use of hypnotherapy with clients with communication disorders. It is thus aimed mainly at speech therapists. Chapter 6 is likewise aimed at physiotherapists and in some parts would be useful to other professionals such as nurses and occupational therapists. The contents for Chapter 7 was the focus of much deliberation and discussion. We make no apology for our final choice which includes the use of hypnosis for clients with a non-medically related wish to lose weight, and for excessive smokers. The justification for creating another short chapter lay in the fact that the conditions did not easily fit under the titles of other chapters and yet they are frequently met in health care work. For example, back pain is exacerbated by overweight, excessive smoking can precipitate and/or exacerbate voice disorders, etc.

We are confident that this book will be a very useful source book and training handbook for members of the Health Care Professions. We recommend, however, that those intending to acquire and use hypnotherapy skills consider attending formal training since a book can not provide the considerable practical skills needed for effective practice.

*S. Abudarham, MSc, LCST, MCST, DipCST*
*Editor*
Birmingham, United Kingdom.
1991

## ACKNOWLEDGEMENTS

I acknowledge the help and advice given to me by my colleague Lorna Povey. I also acknowledge the help given by Christine Yates who typed Chapter 6, and my wife Shirley for typing the rest of the manuscript and its countless drafts.

*Part I –*

# Theoretical Issues

# CHAPTER 1
# The Phenomenon

## Samuel Abudarham

### Historical Overview

Most textbooks on hypnosis discuss at varying lengths the history of hypnosis and its relevance. Hartland (1971) and Rowley (1986) give such an account, as does Heap (1988). It is, therefore, not necessary to give an in depth account in this book but an overview would be appropriate, if only because many of the current myths and popular fears and misconceptions find their roots in historical antecedents.

The phenomenon has been known to the world, under one name or another, for centuries. Some have argued that Biblical personalities such as Moses and Jesus Christ may unwittingly, or knowingly, have used hypnosis in their ministrations. The term itself comes from the Greek 'hypnos' meaning 'sleep', a term now known to be inaccurate as the 'sleep' and 'hypnotic' phenomenon are very different (See later). The Greek etymology of the term does not itself suggest its origin, but it is known that the Greeks made use of hypnosis. The phenomenon assumed magical properties and was largely used by religious leaders. The association between pagan religious practice and hypnosis exists to this very day, in a century of so called enlightenment. Very often hypnosis was used as part of a more extensive ritual.

The phenomenon has been explained in terms such as, the effect of the stars on the individual and/or mystical and (invisible) magnetic waves. The best known advocator of this theory was a 15th century Swiss physician, Paracelsus. This theory had an impact which was to last some two centuries. Initially, it was elaborated by Van Helmont in the late sixteenth/early seventeenth century. The source of this magnetic influence was now attributed to the human being himself. Physical contact, to many hypnotists then, became an important part of the therapeutic interaction as this would allow the magnetism to radiate from the hypnotist to his subject, thus influencing the latter's mental and physical states. Most readers will have seen stage hypnotists using this approach with their subjects.

The truth of the matter is that physical contact is rarely necessary to induce a hypnotic trance, but for showmen and possible charlatans, it enhances the mystique they like to project and which forms an essential and integral part of a sensational stage act. It is tentatively suggested by this author that many subjects expect such physical contact to take place and unless this 'confidence trick' is played, a degree of scepticism may be engendered.

The term 'animal magnetism' was coined by Van Helmont and the concept was subsequently popularised further by the charismatic eighteenth century Austrian physician, Franz Anton Mesmer. The documentation about Mesmer's work in hypnosis is now legend. His reputation was responsible for contributing new words to the lexicon - 'mesmerise' and 'mesmerism'. Mesmer believed in 'magnet' power and he initially employed actual magnets which he believed could remove the putative blocks in the nervous system caused by astral magnetic fluids and which caused physical and mental dysfunction in individuals. To aid him in this objective, he frequently used an iron rod with which he would touch or stroke the 'patient's' body, or parts thereof.

Through a mixture of professional jealousies and political antagonism, Mesmer had to give his work up in Vienna and moved on to Paris, quickly starting a practice there. It was here that his fame grew to such an extent that in order to cope with the numbers of clients, he started conducting group hypnosis. As his reputation increased so did the suggestibility of those who came for his help. This suggestibility was also enhanced by the rituals Mesmer adopted to conduct his group sessions and the paraphenalia he employed. He skilfully manipulated the treatment environment, thus adding to the mysterious (and mystic) element of the proceedings. The unsuspecting subjects were introduced to a dimly lit room whose windows were thickly curtained. There were also mirrors and background music.

In the middle of the room was a large 'baquet', a barrel-type structure (some authors report the presence of several 'baquets'). Subjects were encouraged to grasp one of the many iron rods protruding from the top of the 'baquet' (or sides of the 'baquets') by Mesmer who wore a striking, lilac-coloured, silken robe. The subjects were encouraged to remain silent and hold hands. They were told that the 'baquet' contained magnetised material which included iron filings, powdered glass and water.

Mesmer stood in his magnificence, holding a wand with which he touched his 'patients' simultaneously continuously extolling the benefits of the treatment. Patients could also apply the rods to any ailing parts of their body. Whereas some of these patients did not report any change in themselves, others reacted in bizarre ways and were often reduced to hysterical forms of behaviour - some would fall down and go into convulsions. Far from causing alarm, Mesmer would assure his subjects that such behaviour indicated the success of the treatment. He also used physical contact, the 'placing of the hands', on different parts of the 'patient's' body.

Again, Mesmer's incredible success made him a number of influential enemies within his own profession and in ecclesiastic and political levels. The final 'coup de grace' was administered by the findings of a Royal Commission set up by King Louis XVI. The inability of many so-called scientists to establish a scientific explanation for Mesmer's 'success' was considered proof positive as to its 'charlatanery'. Undoubtedly, prejudice from a Church who, in ignorance of the workings of the phenomenon, could not acknowledge that a human being could have such an effect on others in the absence of some sorcery, together with professional jealousies and unsubstantiated allegations of deceit, immoral practices, and harmful effects of his methods, Mesmer was forced to stop his treatment sessions and was in fact stripped of his licence. But this was not the end of 'animal magnetism' and others continued Mesmer's work, developing and investigating new theories and novel strategies.

Perhaps the next most notable practitioner of this 'art' was a Mancunian surgeon called James Braid. He had witnessed a demonstration of hypnotic induction by the French 'magnetiser', La Fontaine, in Manchester, in 1841. An attempt by Braid, there and then, to expose La Fontaine as a charlatan served to prove to him the contrary and he found himself experiencing a trance state. After some experimentation with friends and family, he started inducing trance in patients pre-operatively, so that he conducted some operations having hypnotised his patient and making use of hypnotic analgesia. Braid employed the 'eye fixation' technique to induce a trance. His patients were asked to fix their gaze on a bright object whilst he suggested to them that they would become progressively tired and sleepy. In fact, Braid believed that the patient did enter a form of sleep state, and concluded that the trance was not produced by any 'magnetic fluids'. He thus, called the phenomenon 'neurohypnology' or 'nervous sleep'. The term 'hypnosis' or 'hypnotism' ('hypnos' being the Greek word for 'sleep') became popularised and, though extremely inappropriate since the hypnotic trance is quite dissimilar to the sleeping state, remains in use to date. The trance phenomenon was, he felt, due to suggestion alone to a subject whose suggestibility had been increased artificially. There are many today who feel that this conclusion still holds true.

It took an eminent French neurologist and head of the Saltpetriere Hospital in Paris, Jean Martin Charcot in the last quarter of the nineteenth century, to raise the respectability of hypnosis. This would seem to have occurred more by Charcot's stature and respect with which he was held in the medical world, than by the quality of the work he did. His observations about the effect hypnosis had on patients suffering from hysteria and conversely the possibility of inducing hysterical conditions through hypnosis led him to the subsequently disproved theory that there was a relationship between hypnosis and hysteria.

One of Charcot's most celebrated "pupils" was the founder of psychoanalysis, the Austrian Dr. Sigmund Freud. Having worked under another celebrated medical colleague Joseph Breuer, Freud got interested in hypnosis as a treatment for neurotic conditions. Soon after Breuer ceased using hypnosis with his hysterical patients, Freud went to Paris to study Charcot's work. However, he found several drawbacks in its use, particularly in that not all patients were hypnotisable. At that time he had started developing his psychoanalytic techniques and soon gave up the use of hypnosis in favour of psychoanalysis.

The twentieth century witnessed two further personalities in the field of hypnosis, both of whom, by their 'scientific' approach to their work, were to influence the course and use of hypnotherapy. These were Clark Hull and

Milton Erickson. Of these two, Erickson, who died in 1980, is the one who has made the most impact on some of the views held today on the nature and practice of hypnosis. Aspects of his work are referred to later on in this chapter and elsewhere in this book. An interesting critical perspective on Erickson and his work is given by McCue (1988).

## Can hypnosis be defined

There are several issues which need to be considered to answer this question. First, does a 'hypnotic state' actually exist? Whatever the answer, what does one have to do to enter or be induced into the 'state'? How does this state come about and what are the pre-requisites for its achievement? What does one experience when in this state?

It is not easy to define a hypnotic state and it is an indisputable fact that different subjects will describe their experience in different ways. Very often reports of such experiences will depend on factors such as their preconceived ideas of what the trance will be like, their ability to verbalise their experiences, the depth which the trance has reached and so on. Some subjects find it very difficult to tell whether they have achieved a hypnotic state or not. This can happen when the experience does not match their expectations. Equally so, patients may deny having experienced a trance state because it either does not conform with the perception of what it should have felt like or because the experience has not fitted with what the hypnotherapist may have explained it would be.

The preliminaries of any first contact must include discussion of the subject's perceptions of hypnosis, as will be seen later. This is perhaps one of the major reasons for discussing definitions of hypnosis. It is all too easy for the hypnotherapist to disregard the patient's account of his experience simply because it may not conform with the text book definition of the trance.

A quick review of the current literature would indicate that there is not a consensus definition of 'hypnosis' nor about what the phenomenon consists of. The descriptions and definitions offered are very often influenced by schools of psychological and perhaps to an extent, neuropsychological thought.

## 'Sleep' v. hypnotic state

For some time and up to the early 50s, the 'hypnotic' state had been considered synonymous with the 'sleep' state. As early as 1785, an anonymously published pamphlet described the trance state as "an intermediate state between sleep and wakefulness, which has the characteristics of both, and produces the greatest number of phenomena which belong to neither." Gibson (1977) comments that had the author not used this to describe what he referred to as "magnetism", many would generally agree that this is a reasonable description of a trance state.

Early studies using primitive electroencephalographs (EEG) led many to believe that hypnosis was the same as sleep. Later studies employing more advanced EEG techniques (in Evans, 1972) indicated that the physiological state as suggested by the patterns of brainwaves of the hypnotised and sleeping person were not the same. However, many studies were handicapped because not enough was known about the nature of sleep.

It has been recognised that there are at least five recognisable states of sleep each producing a different EEG pattern producing rhythms of different cycles per second. The more relaxed and first stage before going to sleep produced alpha rhythm (8-12 cps) which were typical of any relaxed state whether followed by sleep or not. An interesting stage (fifth) during the sleep phase may occur at certain intervals. It is characterised by rapid eye movements (REM) of the eyeballs under closed eyelids. These intervals produced the highest level of brain activity which could reach between 12 - 20 cps (beta rhythm). Subjects awoken during this phase reported they have been experiencing dreams. Whereas REM sleep, often referred to as 'paradoxical' sleep, may have some similarities in its EEG patterns to stage one sleep, it is much more difficult to wake subjects from REM sleep.

As the technology in EEG recordings was refined, further studies indicated that hypnotised patients, unless they fell asleep, demonstrated alpha rhythms and were in a special state of relaxation, and not asleep, but these contained variations not found in the relaxed states/phases of sleep or wakefulness. Furthermore, changes in brain activity were demonstrated when subjects were in a somnambulistic stage or when experiencing hallucinations, which were quite different to the brain activity of deep sleep and actual perceptual experiences when awake, respectively.

Thus, whereas there may be similarities in brain activity in the first phase of sleep (alpha rhythms) and hypnosis, there would seem to be great differences in EEG recordings in the hypnotic state and stages 2 and 3 of sleep. No delta rhythms (fourth sleep phase) have been observed in hypnotised subjects. This stage of sleep is the deepest and the most difficult to wake from.

Two important conclusions could be made in the light of these findings. One was that 'an altered state' did occur during hypnosis which was not only psychological but also physiological and furthermore the latter was measurable. Other physiological signs can also take place, some readily observable, during a trance state and these include changes in the make-up of the blood chemistry and pressure, respiration, heart rate, perspiration response reflexive and even voluntary movements.

There is, however, still some resistance to those drawing similarities between sleep and hypnotic states. Some, such as Marcuse (1982) and Rowley (1986) argue that physiological changes would be determined by different induction techniques. Those techniques emphasising 'sleep' may well produce physiological activity similar to those found in real sleep states but other techniques emphasising wakefulness would not. Others have used this argument to explain why EEGs in hypnotised individuals may be similar to stage one of the sleep state. Conclusions based on EEG recordings may also be suspect as electronic machines are very susceptible to picking up a variety of ambient noises and other conditions which may influence their readings.

Other contrasts have been drawn between sleep and hypnotic states. If a subject falls asleep whilst in hypnosis without being encouraged verbally to do so by the hypnotist, it could well be because he is very tired and the relaxing atmosphere is conducive to a welcome and probably needed snooze. When the subject wakes up he will report that at some point he did not hear the hypnotist talking to him nor was aware of any other stimulus. He knows he has been asleep and has no awareness of what has transpired during that time. Whereas a hypnotised subject may experience 'amnesia' for some experiences, when he wakes up he can often indicate an awareness that he was in a trance and not asleep.

An interesting phenomenon is that of 'alert' trance. Whereas this state is not considered to be a type of 'sleep' state, it has been described more as a type of 'reverie' or 'daydreaming' state. The induction of the alert trance has been studied by Vingoe (1968). The subject is not asked to relax and become 'sleepy' or 'drowsy' but encouraged to concentrate on a single idea, and by doing so enter the (alert) trance.

In conclusion, the arguments for and against equating sleep with hypnosis will most likely continue but the present general consensus is that there may be some similarities but that both states are different. It is interesting to note that some present day hypnotists still use terminology during clinical sessions such as 'deep sleep', 'you will awake', the latter phrase suggesting that the subject will be brought out of a 'sleep' state.

## 'Hypnotic state' theories

The experience of the nature of a hypnotic state can not be described using one criterion. There are likely to be several factors such as how quickly one enters a trance state and the nature and extent of responses to suggestions such as eye closure, arm heaviness and levitation, response to post hypnotic suggestion and so on. There would seem to be a correlation between many of these.

In trying to define hypnosis, one can not avoid discussing what has to happen for a hypnotic state to be achieved. Many theories have been proposed among which was Janet's theory of dissociation (1925). Janet regarded the artificially produced state of hypnosis as a condition of dissociation so that one part of the mind functioned independently from others. An example of this was manifested when a subject under hypnosis could recall experiences of which he is generally unaware when in a normal waking state. Similarly, subjects could be encouraged to forget experiences, under a trance state, which they would normally be aware of when awake. This claim has to be evaluated considering the possibilities that the so-called 'recall' could be a reflection of subject's fantasies and forgetfulness as a result of the subject's reluctance to divulge personal experiences. It may sometimes happen that subjects interpret, or misinterpret what they think are the expectations of the hypnotherapist, and respond accordingly, claiming experiences which fit in with these expectations.

A development from Janet's dissociation theory was the one proposed by Hilgard (1973) and others, and often referred to as the neo-dissociation theories. Hilgard does not refute the possibility of physiological mechanisms being involved in the hypnotic phenomenon. He believes, however, that the hypnotic subject enters an altered state of consciousness and not a sleep state. In the former, a subconscious, or as Hilgard calls it, a 'hidden observer' functions independently from a conscious part. Through suggestion under hypnosis, a hypnotist is able to communicate with the hidden part which in turn responds without the conscious part being aware. Partial or complete 'communication' between both parts does however, sometimes take place, the results of which can have a variety of effects on the subject. This theory explains how under hypnosis subjects can do things that they would not be aware of during a wake state. Whereas psychological theories of hypnosis seem to have predominated in the literature, physiological attributes of hypnosis have been considered for over a century, and are still witnessed in the current literature.

Having briefly reviewed different recent explanations of the hypnosis phenomenon, Waxman (1981) concluded that there was both a psychological and neurophysiological component. He thus defined the hypnotic state as "an altered state of awareness effected by total concentration on the voice of the therapist. It will result in measurable physical, neurophysiological and psychological changes in which may be produced distortion of emotion, sensation, image and time."

This definition would seem to very briefly and albeit simplistically, refer to the questions posed at the beginning of this section.

## Does a hypnotic state exist?

Other theories of the hypnosis phenomenon belong to a paradigm which, whilst not necessarily rejecting that an altered state of consciousness may exist, rejects the traditional notion that it is due to a hypnotic state arguing that a subject's behaviour can be accounted through non-hypnosis related explanations.

One such theory found a strong advocate in Barber (1969). He argued that behaviour sometimes explained as due to a subject acting under hypnosis was in fact a result of 'task motivation'. The subjects in fact had been motivated to execute a task because of very strong suggestion or following subjection to strong pressure by an individual, usually one in authority. Subjects could thus be coerced into exhibiting a behaviour or even report a covert (mental) experience which would fit the stated views or expectations of the authority figure. This author has experienced such behaviour but suspects that in many cases, such subjects have in fact not achieved even a light trance. Furthermore, if as some authors have reported, many subjects retain different levels of independence from the hypnotist's suggestions, it is not inconceivable that even in a trance (or prior to entering one) some subjects may decide to report what they think the hypnotist wants to hear. In a therapeutic relationship it is not unknown for this to happen and many patients do not wish to 'disappoint' their therapist.

Spanos (1982) who had collaborated with Barber, developed the 'role-playing' theory further and advanced the view that hypnotic behaviour is not unlike social behaviours in that it is goal-directed, purposeful and self-initiated. A similar theory had been proposed earlier by White in 1941. Responses by the subject are not involuntary and he interprets them as voluntary. The subject achieves the goal set by the hypnotist's suggestions by fantasising how they would be achieved in a wake state. Furthermore, the subject's behaviour is determined by the way he perceives hypnotic behaviour to be.

A similar view held by social psychologists such as Sarbin and Coe (1972) includes the notion that a social interaction takes place between hypnotist and subject in which the former suggests a role and the latter acts it out. The ability of the subject to enter a role is not dissimilar to play acting or even to an audience empathising with a role acted by a theatrical or film star. Theories such as these are hard to substantiate when one considers that painless surgery is possible under hypnosis - a hard role to 'act'! Furthermore, whereas results of studies comparing subjects acting as if they were hypnotised and hypnotised subjects have not been unequivocable, naive observers have noted certain characteristics which have differentiated between these two groups.

One of these arguments is based on laboratory observations (Orne, 1962) that subjects under hypnosis employ 'trance logic' such as transparent hallucinations. The phenomenon is manifested by subjects being able to perceive objects whose view is 'supposedly' screened by another hallucinated object. Subjects simulating hypnosis would report that they are not able to describe or imagine objects shielded from view by other imagined objects.

The theory that the subject responds to the 'hypnotist' not because the former has entered a trance state but because he wishes to 'comply' with the 'hypnotist's' suggestions, has been advanced by Wagstaff (1981). In complying, the subject does not need to share all the hypnotist's views though he may accept or believe some of them. Responses by the subject are therefore brought about by his 'compliance' with, and/or belief in the realisation of the hypnotist's instructions. If the subject does not experience what is being suggested by the hypnotist, he will make it happen by using his own imagination or by pretence. If he does experience a suggestion, he will believe that he is bringing it about himself.

## Other theories

It is not within the scope of this book to explore other theories in detail. However, in order that the reader is given an awareness that there are others, a small selection of those mentioned in the literature are briefly reviewed below.

One very common view has been that subjects who can be hypnotised are 'hypersuggestible'. This theory was mainly influenced by the work of

Liebeault in 1860, and later Bernheim (1886) and Forel (1956). Current opponents of this view argue that this suggests that a hypnotised subject has no will of his own and is at the mercy of the hypnotist and his suggestions. It is felt that this is a dangerous view to hold, especially since it perpetuates the popular myth of the all-powerful hypnotist.

Behaviourists have argued that hypnosis occurs as a result of 'conditioning'. The conditioners are mainly the words used during the induction process. Pavlov's work (1923) in animal hypnosis prompted him and his followers to draw parallels with hypnosis in humans. Hypnosis, they concluded, depended on the thinking part of the brain (the cortex) being 'inhibited' thus allowing the more susceptible primitive centres of the brain to take control. Partial inhibition, as manifested when subjects maintained the ability to be mentally and physically active, was due to the state of excitation of 'sentinel points'. These remain receptive to suggestions made by the hypnotist and, though unaware of other stimuli in the environment, the subject can be made acutely aware of any stimuli suggested by the hypnotist. Pavlov viewed the hypnotic state as a form of sleep state, and this has been said to have influenced many other researchers in considering hypnosis and sleep as the same states.

It is not just the 'classical conditioning' paradigm that has been applied to hypnosis but also the 'operant', or 'instrumental' conditioning associated with Skinner. In this case, the verbal conditioning takes place after the behaviour is performed such as in the postural sway task when the subject is assured by the experimenter that he is indeed falling forwards, just as soon as the latter observes the slightest forward sway by the subject.

Meares' 'Atavistic theory' (1960) was based on Pavlov's. In hypnosis, he explained, the mental functions of the subject regress to a more primitive and suggestible level so that ideas are accepted uncritically and more readily. Gibson (op.cit.) concludes that when one is awake, one is constantly evaluating external stimuli critically and in doing so is 'reality testing'. This personal reality is determined by factors such as one's beliefs, attitudes and expectations. During the sleep state, one is hardly affected by outside stimuli but instead one may be affected by inner ones which revolve around past experiences. Whilst in this state, very little, if any, critical evaluation takes place and dreams are often accepted uncritically even though they may occur in confused states. During a hypnotic induction, a subject is deprived from going to sleep by the constant talk from the hypnotist. The subject however, allows the hypnotist to conduct a lot of the 'reality testing' but does not completely give up his critical faculty. Any trance-induced hallucinations, for example, are dealt with by the subject in the same way as he deals with similar experiences during the sleep state.

Finally, a word about the psychoanalytic theory. This states that in hypnosis, a regression takes place and the 'ego' takes control. The 'ego' is responsible for the loss of contact with reality so that many suppressed experiences can more easily be revealed. It is the 'ego' which can initiate and terminate this loss of contact. Before this can happen however, the patient must be able to enjoy a positive transference with the hypnotherapist (in non-psychoanalytic terms, a 'good relationship') who in turn is then able to manipulate the patient's thought processes. It would seem clear that whereas the study of the nature of hypnosis and its correlates has developed extensively over the last two decades, there is no unequivocal consensus of opinion. Perhaps the most important issue in our present state of knowledge lies with the subject's perception of whether he has achieved a hypnotic state, his description of such a state and how effective hypnosis is to enhance the quality of his life.

## Subjective perceptions

What then do subjects report has been their own experiential perception of the hypnotic experience? There are too many to mention but among the most common in this author's experience have been a slight prevailing sense of wariness particularly in the first experience. As patients have developed more confidence and the fear of the unknown recedes, they report a feeling of relaxation, sometimes unprecedented. Some feel they have found themselves 'floating', others have reported a sense of 'heaviness' affecting the whole or parts of the body, even parts not mentioned by the hypnotist as part of an induction technique. A sense of being 'dragged down' or 'quickly sliding down' is often reported. (One patient described this feeling using one word — whoosh!) It is hard sometimes to say to what extent the pre-hypnosis discussion influences such reports. Most patients have reported that they can hear everything said to them by the hypnotist and many, though not all, will admit to being aware of environmental sounds. Not every patient feels he is powerless to ignore the hypnotist's suggestion and the majority have in fact felt able to in certain circumstances.

Many patients have reported that they are able to modify the hypnotist's suggestions and still achieve similar goals. One patient for example was asked to achieve relaxation by imagining themselves lying on a beach under a 'red hot' sun. Perceiving the aim of such an imaginary panorama but disliking such intense heat, the patient imagined himself lying on grass by a cool brook. Very often lapses of concentration on the hypnotist's voice are reported by clients.

The feeling that they can come out of hypnosis before the hypnotist suggests it is not shared by all patients. Very often surprise is reported at their responses under hypnosis, particularly when arm-levitation or rigidity is experienced, and perhaps more dramatically a successful response to a post-hypnotic suggestion that following a certain stimulus, the patient will enter hypnosis even though a week or more has elapsed.

So much of these experiences are determined by factors such as the patient's motivation, understanding of the phenomenon, trust in the hypnotist, and so on, that it is not easy to determine a commonality of most of these experiences for all patients.

## The nature of 'suggestion'

No matter which theory of hypnosis one espouses, there is one undisputed fact and that is that the phenomenon is brought about by 'suggestion', verbal or non verbal, and usually by another person. Sometimes situations on their own can achieve the same phenomenon (Christie and Phillips, 1988). The basic characteristic of 'suggestion' is that it seeks to influence a subject's behaviour, often through non-rational means (c.f. 'persuasion') – one wonders whether the same can be said of 'auto-suggestion', as may be used in self hypnosis.

Some authors have classified different types of suggestions and studied their relative therapeutic effect (see below). Eysenck distinguished between 'primary' and 'secondary' suggestions. Primary suggestions are themselves 'hypnosis-like' suggestions of the type often employed in hypnotic induction techniques. For example, a subject may be asked to hold a pendulum hanging at the end of a piece of string, in front of him. Through suggestion, the pendulum may begin to swing ostensibly of its own accord. Similarly, a primary suggestion may involve or require some muscular activity such as arm rigidity. Secondary suggestions were the type which played on a subject's gullibility in a wake state. Contrasts have been similarly drawn between 'direct' and 'indirect' suggestion. In the former, the subject is told emphatically what he is going to experience, and in the latter, the suggestion is more open-ended and of the type which 'permits' the subject to make up his own mind, or indicates that its realisation may occur.

One of the best known advocators of 'indirect' suggestion was Erickson. He and Rossi (1980) have argued that indirect suggestion is more effective than 'direct' suggestion because it evades conscious criticism and thereby makes it easier for patients to accept. A 'suggestion' may be evaluated critically or not by the subject though if a good relationship exists with the hypnotist, the subject may accept suggestion on faith.

Another contrast has been made relating to suggestion made by prestigious people and those made by people without prestige i.e. 'prestige' and 'non-prestige' suggestion. Hull (1933) argued that suggestions made by a hypnotist who the subject considers has prestige would have a greater effect on the subject's response to hypnosis. A subject's ability to enter a trance does often depend on certain interactive criteria. It is more likely that a subject will more readily and quickly enter a trance if he has respect and trust in the hypnotist. As these develop, subjects are likely to find it easier to enter a trance. However, the hypnotist's 'prestige' has not been found to make any difference.

## Suggestibility, hypnotisability and susceptibility

Much has been written about how and whether 'suggestibility', 'hypnotisability' and 'susceptibility' may be prerequisites for successfully and speedily entering a hypnotic trance. The differences between them has not always been clear, nor have their implications for different aspects of the hypnosis phenomenon and its therapeutic uses. Even in recent literature, one sometimes finds that these terms have been employed indiscriminately, particularly where 'hypnotisablity' and 'susceptibility' are being discussed. These two terms are often used interchangeably or exclusively.

Whether 'hypnotisability' and 'susceptibility' are the same phenomenon, or whether they are related, is often not clear. The problem is exacerbated by their intangibility. Measures of these attributes largely depend on the 'measurer's' view of what they comprise. When it is claimed that a test measures 'hypnotisablity', to what extent might it be measuring parameters of 'susceptibility' as well? Does one have to be 'susceptible' before being 'hypnotisable'? After all, unless a subject has been truly hypnotised, one can not be certain that he is susceptible no matter what predictive tests of susceptibility have indicated. Are there in fact, any distinguishing features and can these be measured? The following overview of the literature relates to this vast, and sometimes all-consuming subject. Its value lies because it relates to issues not only queried by researchers and clinicians, but it is also a source of anxiety for patients, particularly in their first encounter with a hypnotist.

'Suggestibility' refers to the extent to which a subject will readily accept suggestion. Some have argued that the degree of 'suggestibility' is an important factor which could determine phenomenona such as how quickly a subject may enter a trance state, the depth to which it can be taken and how effective post-hypnotic suggestion will be.

It is possible that some subjects are more suggestible than others, but suggestibility also depends on a subject's perception of hypnosis, his motivation, whether he relates to the hypnotist and other factors already mentioned. In addition to these, there will be variations among subjects on their ability to become involved in the recollection of fantasies invoked by the therapist or indeed generated by the subjects themselves. The success with which subjects are able to achieve this involvement may also depend on their ability to accept such suggestions. It seems clear that during a hypnotic trance, subjects are in a state of heightened suggestibility but this by no means implies that they will respond to all suggestions made by the hypnotist (this matter is discussed further on).

In the past, there was a mistaken view that certain personality traits, for example weak will, favoured suggestibility. It is clear that even very strong willed individuals can be highly suggestible if their co-operation is forthcoming or if suggestions are made in ways acceptable to them and which do not threaten their autonomy. Those, such as dissociation theorists, who adhere to the operation of a hierarchical system of conscious states during trance states would propose that suggestions are input into an uncritical level of conscious, sometimes referred to as the 'subconscious'. The critical 'conscious' is by-passed and so the subject will respond more readily to suggestions, often whether they are rational (to the 'conscious' mind) or not. The trance state thus produces a higher level of suggestibility.

Given that 'suggestiblity' is not a unitary entity and as discussed above depends on other factors, it is not easy to see how it can be reliably measured. However, many studies purporting to measure suggestibility have been published. Weitzenhoffer and Hilgard (1959), developed the well known 'Stanford Hypnotic Susceptibility Scale'. The fact that the test comprises 12 items suggests that the authors consider hypnosis not to consist of just one variable.

Many of the studies conducted have been with experimental subjects rather than 'patients' undergoing therapy (Hart, 1988). It has been reported that experimental subjects may respond differently to 'clinical' subjects. Many of the former have been students, an easily obtainable population for researchers. For a variety of reasons that can not be discussed here, this group may differ in their attitudes, motivation, degree of compliance etc. from clinical subjects, and this may yield different results. Thus, to what extent suggestion is effective in clinical work (as opposed to experimental) is not always easy to evaluate, since the consequence may not be immediate. This has been seen in patients who immediately after a course of hypnotherapy may claim that hypnosis has not helped them and several weeks or months later may report that they have successfully resolved their problem but deny that hypnotherapy had influenced this recovery.

Any claims that degrees of suggestibility may determine the ease or speed with, or depth to which hypnosis can be achieved, have to be scrutinised in order to establish how suggestibility was measured and what type of suggestions were employed. Eysenck in 1943, and in a replicated study conducted with Furneaux two years later (1945), concluded that his initial findings indicated that only 'primary' suggestibility correlated highly with susceptibility and this was confirmed by the replicated study, and subsequently by other researchers.

Hart (1985; 1988) reports on a study he was conducting with clinical subjects undergoing therapy. Early results indicated that subjects receiving 'direct' suggestion were 'doing somewhat better overall' in their treatment than those receiving indirect suggestion, though they were all progressing. His results also indicated that whereas highly hypnotisable subjects did better than the lower ones with direct suggestion, hypnotisability was not significantly affected when indirect suggestion was employed.

In a study involving hypnotic analgesia, Fricton and Roth (1985) arrived at a similar conclusion for subjects given direct suggestion but they found that indirect suggestion favoured subjects with low susceptibility. Can it be that low susceptibility subjects are so because they maintain their critical faculties to a greater extent than more susceptible subjects. The former may be more wary about losing their independence to the hypnotist and may be more responsive to a type of suggestion which allows them a certain amount of choice, as Erickson and Rossi (op. cit.) have argued. This author's experience suggests that this is not always so. On occasions even subjects who have entered a very deep trance may also experience an anxiety that they will lose their independence to the hypnotist.

The term 'hypnotisability' refers to how easily, quickly and deeply a subject can be hypnotised. The term 'susceptibility' would suggest an inherent or even acquired characteristic. Some authors (Udolf, 1981; Rowley, op. cit.) have attributed a personality characteristic to a person's 'susceptibility' and this in turn determines his 'hypnotisability'.

There have been many studies conducted, notably by Hilgard, to explore 'susceptibility'. One of the questions often asked is whether a higher level of suggestibility implies a greater susceptibility. Gibson (op. cit.) has reported that experiments to establish a positive correlation between these have disappointed experimenters.

Several studies have shown that there is a great difference in the susceptibility of subjects not only in how quickly they can be trance-induced but also in the depth of trance that can be achieved. Some authors have suggested that people are less susceptible today than perhaps a century ago. This may be due to the simpler life style and a lesser scientifically aware society of the time.

Hilgard (1970) has suggested that susceptibility may be partly dependent on the whole process of a subject growing up in different environments and his interaction with patients and others. One of her most interesting findings was that adults who had been severely punished in their childhood were more susceptible than those who had not had this experience.

Whereas the popular concept, especially perpetuated by the cinema, is that females are more hypnotisable than males, there would seem to be little evidence of this, to date. Gibson (op. cit.) claims that in fact sex differences have been reported favouring females in terms of their susceptibilty but that researchers have negated such differences because they were not statistically significant. He argues that 'non-significance' is merely a mathematician's statistical concept relating to the chance factor and that data found not to be statistically significant does not negate its existence, especially when the phenomenon has been reported in several studies, though albeit as 'statistically non-significant'.

Among the correlates of susceptibility and hypnotisability are the ability of a patient to absorb himself in imaginative and fantasy thoughts. Wagstaff (1988) states that imaginative involvement is not necessary as a prerequisite to hypnotisability as evidenced by subject's ability to respond contrary to their imaginings. Neuropsychological correlates are briefly reviewed by Gruzelier (1988). He concludes that dominant left hemisphere subjects are particularly susceptible since the common introduction to many induction techniques employs visual fixation, a process controlled by the left hemisphere. As the subject enters the suggestive state, the 'critical' left hemisphere then gives way to the more 'amenable' right hemisphere. Following a very brief review of studies of physiological correlates, Rowley (op. cit.) concluded that "no physiological measures seem to have been isolated which reliably predict hypnotisability." He tentatively acknowledges the possibility that handedness, gender and EEG alpha activity may.

Other parameters have been considered in relation to susceptibility. Waxman (op. cit.) considers 'age' and recommends that "children under the age of seven and adults over the age of 70 should be excluded" thus suggesting a reduced hypnotisability in these individuals. Authors such as London (1965) and Marcuse (op. cit.) state that children between the ages of seven to fourteen are said to be more hypnotisable. Susceptibility would seem to decrease somewhat after this age.

To what extent the variation could be due to psychological and/or physiological correlates of age rather than age itself is not clear. There is always some danger of considering biological as opposed to 'mental' age as a correlate especially since many other correlates of hypnosis studied depend more on 'mental' age than on biological age. In this author's experience, much has depended on whether he and the young subject have known each other (e.g. socially) before the therapy encounter so that children as young as five and a half years of age who were previously known by him were easier to hypnotise than those not previously known. One has to presume that familiarity and trust were important factors especially when dealing with patients rather than (experimental) subjects.

Perhaps the most popular correlate studied has been personality traits. It is hard to give credence to any positive results of such studies since there are so many diverse, and sometimes opposing, operational definitions of 'personality', and many approaches to its assessment. The fact is that most studies have indicated either no relationship or very small correlations between personality traits and susceptibility. What remains a question is to what extent personality or situational variables (McCue, op. cit.) or indeed the cumulative effect of such factors, and not just the type of suggestion used, might determine a subject's hypnotisability and/or susceptibility. One factor which could be attributed to personality, but also depends very much on situational criteria is the subject's attitudes and motivation. Not unexpectedly, subjects with positive attitudes and motivation have been found to be more hypnotisable.

One is very aware that having studied this subsection, the reader might retort "so what?". How useful is all this information to the practitioner? Does one need to waste time considering or measuring such correlates before one can decide on whether hypnotherapy is indicated? The answers probably are that given the state of the art (or science) some studies are so inconclusive that they do not have any reliable or practical value. Others which may be more conclusive may relate to correlates which are no easier a measure of hypnotisability than finding out through the pragmatic approach of attempting to induce a trance in a client. After all, is this not the acid test and objective?

For clinical purposes therefore, many will argue that susceptibility tests, or any consideration of factors such as EEG patterns, handedness, etc., are a waste of time. As Waxman (op. cit.) and Rowley (op. cit.) say, this sort of enquiry and appraisal may have its strengths in the experimental field. Where perhaps it may have clinical implications is in their possible use for predicting 'trance-depth potential' (my term) in clients and as Gruzelier (op. cit.) argues, in how such findings may be able to suggest improved methods of induction and hypnotherapy techniques.

## Can anyone be hypnotised?

But having concluded thus the question is often asked, are all subjects hypnotisable? This is an important question because a client will almost invariably ask, if not wonder, whether he is going to be able to enter a trance.

Hartland (op. cit.) states that 90 per cent of the population can be hypnotised though he stresses that it is likely that the other 10 per cent which one particular hypnotist is unable to hypnotise is likely to be hypnotisable by another who in turn will not be able to hypnotise a different 10 per cent. It would seem from this therefore, that the hypnotist himself may contribute to the hypnotisability of a subject. And yet some authors such as Gibson will state that the capacity to achieve hypnosis depends more on the client/subject than the hypnotist himself. Hypnotists do not vary in their 'power' to hypnotise as an ability to use the technique rather than personal talent distinguishes how good the hypnotist is.

The percentage figures of subjects reported to be insusceptible or unhypnotisable varies so much that one has to wonder whether appropriate steps were taken before concluding that a subject fell into these categories. It is an acknowledged fact that some subjects while not responding to one hypnotist may be more successful with another. It is also accepted that some subjects may not be able to enter a trance state on the first attempt. Marcuse (op. cit.) reports that in one case, 300 hours were required. Equally so, some subjects may not respond to a particular induction technique but may respond to another. Much of the literature reporting suggested incidences of inhypnotisability is lacking in reporting this type of information, thus making any claims difficult to evaluate.

## Can any hypnotisable subject be induced into deep trance?

Another issue discussed in the literature is the number of subjects in the general population who can be expected to enter different depths of trance. Marcuse (op. cit.) gives some approximate figures. He concludes that about 5 to 20 per cent of subjects are able to achieve a somnambulistic level, 60 to 90 per cent are capable of entering a light or medium trance and 5 - 20 per cent are not at all susceptible to hypnosis. He does not consider, as Hartland did, that the particular hypnotist may be an important criterion. He does acknowledge however, that these figures would have to be revised for the more hypnotisable population between the ages of seven and fourteen. These figures are generally agreed by others but their practical usefulness is very doubtful. Furthermore, there are many factors that need to be considered before their validity is accepted, not least how effective the hypnotist is and how reliable reports from subjects about whether they were hypnotised, and if so how deeply, can be considered.

From the clinical point of view, such odds matter little to the client who finds it difficult to enter a trance state or for that matter, to the hypnotist who has not been able to induce such a state. To what extent these figures have been corroborated by the results of properly conducted and valid susceptibility tests, or as is more likely, through anecdotal evidence, is not clear.

It should be noted that the existence of insusceptible subjects resulted in Freud's disenchantment with hypnotherapy and in the development of his own techniques of psychoanalysis.

## Can susceptibility be measured?

Gibson (op. cit.) has stated that "there are no very obvious advance indicators as to whether a person will be susceptible to hypnosis." However, several batteries of tests of susceptibility have been developed, notably by Hilgard, and some of these are described in Chapter 2 of this book.

## Hypnoanalysis and hypnotherapy

Hypnoanalysis is the term given for the use of hypnosis to establish or investigate cause and effect relationships usually of clients' behaviour which may or may not form part of or be a clinical problem. The technique has in its rationale the theory that anyone's behaviour, maladaptive or otherwise has its roots in previous experiences. Memories of such experiences are not always accessible during a waking state. The reason for this could merely be natural forgetfulness though many schools of thought would attribute this forgetfulness to suppression. In the latter case, an individual may find some memories so traumatic that in order to maintain a healthy mental and possibly physical state, he has to suppress such memories. On occasions, however, suppression is not entirely successful and the individual may develop psychological or psychosomatic problems. The objective of hypnoanalysis is to help the individual, through various means and under a trance, reveal and identify such memories which give him an insight into the cause of his current problem, and with therapy be helped to understand its roots. Very often early experiences may influence the way one behaves in the future but whereas such experiences might have been very significant and traumatic when they occurred, factors such as time, maturity, modified attitudes, etc., may allow the individual to rationalise their impact in a different light and thereby cope with them better. It is often the case that the client's successful recall of related memories can also help the therapist to understand his problems and suggest ways to resolve them.

Some of the techniques employed will be briefly described in Chapter 3 and these include regression analysis, hypnopictography and structured dream analysis. They all aim to facilitate for the client, the recall and sometimes re-enactment of suppressed experiences. A client's response during hypnoanalysis is sometimes quite dramatic and is often accompanied by extreme levels of emotional expression, from uncontrolled crying to verbal aggression. Physical aggression is sometimes manifested. Though these extremes are not always the case, it is usually quite impossible to predict a particular client's response. Whether clients are going to benefit from this approach largely depends on the skill of the hypnotherapist which in turn is determined by his knowledge and clinical experience of the condition he is treating. Hartland (op. cit.) has stated that "recall of causal experiences does not always lead to cures of the condition being treated". He cautions that "it is not just what is recalled that is of primary importance, but the use we make of it in order to benefit the patient."

It is for this reason that hypnoanalytic techniques should be used with due caution and never in ignorance of the psychodynamics involved. It should also be borne in mind that sometimes, without any attempt by the hypnotist to do so, some clients can regress themselves during a trance state, particularly when it is being induced by asking clients to imagine themselves somewhere or doing something in particular. As the client is entering a fantasy or role, this experience may trigger long forgotten memories of earlier years. This particular rationale for hypnoanalysis is probably the most common one expounded. Its basis is found predominantly in psychoanalytic theory.

Hartland (op. cit.) advocates that hypnoanalysis should only be used by therapists with a good knowledge of abnormal psychology and the necessary psychoanalytic training and experience, particularly since they need to be competent at dealing with phenomena such as resistance and transference.

If a client demonstrates the latter, he may transfer deep seated emotions of love or hate felt for others to the therapist. Unless properly handled, such reactions may render any therapeutic benefit impossible and worse still could lead to grave repercussions. Hartland states, however, that when hypnoanalytic techniques are employed to help the patient recall buried memories of traumatic experiences, a psychotherapeutic training is less essential. He advises that it is safest to use these techniques for diagnostic purposes only and they should be "shunned altogether as therapeutic instruments."

Some have argued that hypnosis itself is not a therapy. Without wishing to enter into any semantic polemics, it must be said that many clients who have achieved even a light trance and with whom no other therapy technique has been used whilst they have been in hypnosis, often report how well and relaxed they feel after they have woken up. One particular 68 year old lady was questioned on the first session whether she had been hypnotised. As she was making a case to support her view that she had not experienced hypnosis, she suddenly turned to her husband and said "Mind you, that terrible headache I've had all day has gone!" Whether hypnosis on its own is a therapy or not probably has little clinical significance since in most such encounters clearly identifiable therapeutic techniques are employed, whether through just relaxation therapy and/or counselling strategies, and so on. Perhaps the best definition then, of hypnotherapy is the use whilst a client is hypnotised, of any technique aiming to benefit him.

Hypnotherapy may or may not involve hypnoanalysis. If it does, the objective is to help the patient come to terms with and rationalise the memories he is recalling or re-enacting during hypnoanalysis and relating them, if appropriate, to his current problem. The hypnotherapist may encourage the client, if the latter wishes, to verbalise his memories and constantly gives him reassurance and perhaps suggest ways in which the problems could be resolved.

But hypnoanalysis is not always a pre-requisite of hypnotherapy. Many conditions can be treated by other techniques such as hypnotically induced relaxation, ego-strengthening, and most often with as much if not more success.

## Conclusions

Research continues into the nature and applications of hypnosis and is likely to do so well into the next millenium. No doubt claims and counter-claims in this regard will continue for many years, unabated. Hardened researchers will no doubt claim that only results of studies conducted under laboratory conditions can be considered reliable. The fact remains that the conditions found in laboratories, and the subjects studied under such conditions can never entirely reflect the clinical situation and the client seen by the practising hypnotherapist. The only valid clinically applicable conclusions therefore, may only be the ones that the hypnotherapist arrives at in the light of personal clinical experience.

Unfortunately, such conclusions can only lend themselves to a certain degree of generalisation, a fact which is equally true about the validity of applying the results of laboratory research to any other field of clinical practice.

# *Part II* –
# The Practice and Clinical Applications

# CHAPTER 2
# Patient Selection and Preparation

## Samuel Abudarham

Hypnosis has been employed non-clinically and clinically for an infinite number of conditions, from simple relaxation, boosting clients' confidence, enhancing recall by witnesses of a crime, to hypnotically anaesthetising clients pre-surgery. For some time, however, it seemed to be predominantly used for psychological or psychosomatic conditions. There are a small number of hypnotherapists who believe that further research may one day provide evidence for the effective use of hypnosis for organic problems such as space-occupying lesions. This belief may in fact not be as unfeasible as it might seem. The rationale given is that the human being can through the 'power of thought' alter body morphology to some extent. For example, just by pondering on sexually-arousing thoughts (that is, without actually 'seeing' sexually-arousing 'scenes') a man can alter the shape and size of his penis temporarily, through an erection. Similarly, such 'thoughts' set off a whole complex chain of anatomical, physiological and neurological activities and changes, in both man and woman. It is thus, argued that if all this can be brought about through mental activity alone, it may well be possible to harness and direct such activity to bring about neurophysiological activity, and ultimately change, which may, for example, reduce the size of a tumour.

Kroger (1977) quotes an address given by Pendegrass, President to the American Cancer Society, in 1959. The latter stated that he had witnessed cancer patients who had undergone treatment and had lived for years. "We may learn how to influence general body systems and through them modify the neoplasm .... within the body ..... ." Pendegrass suggested that we may find one day that "... within one's mind is a power capable of exerting forces which can either enhance or inhibit progress of this disease."

Kroger (ibid.) briefly reviews some of the work successfully done with cancer patients. One case reported was of a client in her middle forties who had a clinically confirmed brain tumour 'the size of a golf ball'. Under hypnotherapy, she was told to imagine she was playing a game of 'star wars'. She was asked to imagine that the 'battleships' shot missiles at the tumour to destroy it. Several months later, clinical tests showed that the size of the tumour had reduced significantly more than had been expected from the effects of the chemotherapy which had been given.

Whether one finds this case plausible or not should not rule out the possibility that in time hypnotherapy may be used more frequently to help such clinical conditions. After all, 'stress' has been identified as a possible contributing, if not causal factor, for some cancers. No one doubts that hypnotherapy is effective in reducing stress. In Chapter 6, Frazer reports on the use of hypnosis 'to reduce the swelling and bruising accompanying most injuries' by enhancing the circulation to the affected part by hypnotic suggestion. This is again an example of how physiological change can be brought about through hypnosis.

It is not my intention having discussed this issue briefly, to encourage the reader to reach any conclusive decisions about the effectiveness of hypnosis as 'a cure' for tumours, benign or malignant, and no conclusive claims are being made. It would be ill advised and indeed dangerous to suggest as much. On the current state of knowledge, it must certainly not ever be suggested to the patient that hypnotherapy can 'cure' cancers, for example, though hypnotherapy has been shown to be effective in pain control in patients suffering from cancer (see Chapter 6) though not all patients may benefit.

One issue arises, however, if everyone rejects the use of hypnotherapy for such conditions, how are we ever to know whether it may work with some patients or not. This is not just a medical but also a moral issue. Some may argue that hypnotherapy if used at all, should be employed as an adjunct to conventional therapy. Others may advocate hypnotherapy only when orthodox medical intervention has failed. What chance has hypnotherapy got of succeeding in cases when all orthodox medical intervention has failed?

## General considerations

This chapter aims to discuss some fundamental and practical issues relevant to the initial client contact and the criteria for hypnotherapy. Before deciding on any programme of hypnotherapy, the following steps should be taken.

1. Case History and Interview.
2. Establishing if hypnotherapy is indicated as a possible intervention strategy for the client's particular condition, whether as an adjunct to another strategy or on its own.
3. Establishing whether there are any contra-indications to the use of hypnotherapy, as revealed by the client's medical condition.
4. Determining if the condition is outside the hypnotist's professional competence in which case the client should be referred to a professional with an approved qualification to deal with such a condition. On occasions, a collaborative programme with an appropriate professional may be recommended.

Once the decision is made that hypnotherapy is indicated for the condition and that it is within the hypnotist's therapeutic competence, it is very important to establish two other criteria.

5. How motivated and committed is the client to a hypnotherapy programme.
6. How much does the client know about the nature of hypnosis, what benefits is he expecting to gain, and does he have any misconceptions.

Once all this has been established, and the decision has been made that hypnotherapy for the particular client may be beneficial, a typical programme will comprise all or some of the following:

1. Preparation of the client and explanation of the nature of the proposed programme.
2. Induction.
3. Deepening.
4. Establishing an IMR.
5. Ego strengthening.
6. Appropriate Post-hypnotic suggestion.
7. Training in Auto-hypnosis.
8. Termination and awakening.
9. Discussion.
10. Setting goals for the next session.

(Points 2-10 are discussed in detail in Chapter 3)

## Case history and interview

The aims of the case history and interview should address the following:

1. Establishing the reasons why the client may have requested or been referred for hypnosis. An indication of this is often given by determining who referred the client e.g. a physician, another member of the health care profession, etc. For example, if a speech therapist referred the client, the condition may well be related to or indeed be a communication problem. Sometimes, a client may be self-referred. Typical of this type of client is the smoker.

2. It is essential to allow the client to describe his core problem and any related problems, particularly any medical ones. The client should be asked if he is under any medical supervision or treatment. If so, the non-medically qualified hypnotist must ascertain from the client's physician, *in writing,* whether there is any objection, on medical or other grounds, to a programme of hypnosis or hypnotherapy.

The experienced hypnotist can often tell from a properly conducted interview whether the physician's consent needs to be sought. Clues can be obtained by asking the client why he has not asked his physician for help. It may be that some clients do not wish their physician to know that they have requested hypnotherapy. If the hypnotist cannot persuade his client that he should ask for advice from his physician, this wish must be respected but the hypnotist may well decide that he can not proceed. A common scenario is clients who want help to lose weight and may feel they have not had much help from their physician or have not considered it a problem requiring medical help. It may well be that going on a diet may not have any adverse medical repercussion for the client and all he expects from hypnotherapy is an enhanced will power to do so.

Those hypnotists working in the health service may in fact have the client's medical information accessible to them.

3. An interesting approach is to ask the client why he thinks he has the particular problem, what he has done to remedy it and why any attempts to achieve this have failed.

4. Some clients may have had hypnotherapy before. It is helpful to find out whether it was a lay hypnotist or a health care professional practising hypnotherapy. Similarly, it would be very helpful to know what induction techniques had been used, which ones helped and which did not. The answers to these questions may help the hypnotherapist determine the subsequent course of action. It is possible that, as has been suggested in Chapters 1 and 2, a client may not benefit from one hypnotist or induction technique, and might still benefit from another hypnotist or approach.

5. During the interview, the hypnotist should try a holistic approach to the client. Information about the client's social, family and work life would enhance his appreciation of the client as a person. The approach should never be that the hypnotist is confronted by a 'problem in a person' but 'a person with a problem'. An awareness of what makes a client 'tick', what creates stresses, how he deals with life's stresses, which situations does he find relaxing, and which factors exacerbate or relieve the problem, is a prerequisite to any therapeutic intervention. Such information may be incorporated in the programme. For example, a knowledge of a client's hobbies and pastimes could be usefully employed during relaxation routines. Similarly, one should omit using imagery which a client may find disturbing even though such imagery may generally be thought to help other people relax. A typical example is found in a relaxation routine which involves clients imagining themselves going down an escalator. Clients who have a fear of heights may in fact find such imagery very disturbing and even traumatic. It is therefore, pertinent to ask clients if they have any phobias, specifically of heights, water (beach scenes, etc.) or allergies, for example, pollen allergy (garden and countryside scenes).

## Contra-indications

There are many conditions for which hypnotherapy is contra-indicated. Waxman (1989) gives these as 'endogenous depression, schizophrenia, senile, arterio-sclerotic or organic psychosis, alcohol or drug psychosis, pathological personalities, mental subnormality or deficiency, certain physical disorders including thyroid dysfunction, hypoglycaemia and cerebral tumours.'

However, there is not a consensus of opinion with regards to these contra-indications. For example, much has been written about the use of hypnotherapy in the remission of tumours. Waxman (op. cit.) himself acknowledges that schizophrenia has been treated by hypnosis though he sees little justification for this practice since current drug therapy can effectively contain the condition. Whether this is good enough reason for not using hypnosis with schizophrenic patients is very debatable and there will be those 'anti-drug' physicians who might well disagree.

The one caution that must guide all hypnotherapists must be that they do not even contemplate using hypnotherapy for conditions they are not qualified to treat in any other way. This is why the hypnotherapist must establish the exact nature of his client's problems and its possible etiology. This can only be done through a professional liaison with the client's physician and by very carefully obtaining a detailed case history. If the hypnotherapist even suspects that the client's problem or its causality is outside his area of professional competence, the case must not be taken on and must be referred to an appropriate agency. Some readers will argue that this is common practice, whether hypnosis was initially considered as part of the intervention programme or not. This caution does therefore, not apply to such readers. There are however, some grey areas, examples of which are given in Chapter 5.

## Testing client's motivation and commitment

If after careful consideration of all data available and the criteria discussed above, the practitioner decides that the client's condition can be relieved through hypnotherapy, one needs to test the client's motivation and commitment.

This is perhaps the most difficult issue to establish and yet without a client's motivation, it is unlikely that hypnotherapy is going to be effective. It is important to establish that a client *wants* and *believes* in hypnotherapy. If a client has been pressurised to attend, the hypnotist is likely to encounter resistance and even hostility. This may be particularly common with children who are often pressurised to attend by well-meaning parents.

Powerful motivators are related to health, the client's and his family's. Fear of illness and death in the case of overweight and smoking clients is a great motivator. However, motivators expressed sincerely and strongly by clients can lose their impact in a short course of time. When a client who phoned for an appointment was asked why he wanted to give up smoking, he said gravely he had that day buried his mother who had died of cancer and had been a heavy smoker. It was suggested to the client that though this was a great motivator, his decision was perhaps made too near to the tragedy and he should give himself a week and then, if still committed, to phone again and an appointment would be given. He agreed this was a good idea and that was the last heard of him. It was subsequently learned that he had not sought other help and was still smoking.

Very often, it is necessary to obtain a client's commitment by negotiating a 'contract' which can be renewed as appropriate. Some clients expect one session 'to do the trick'. If the hypnotist does not concur, a contract for a minimum number of sessions may need to be negotiated. Similarly, for clients who are likely to become dependent on the hypnotist, a contract may be essential to prevent protracted and unnecessary treatment.

Agreement to 'contract therapy' is perhaps the best indication of a client's motivation. In addition, one should establish that the client wants to get better and what benefits are expected after a course of treatment. Unreasonable expectations should be checked straight away to avoid undue disappointment and possible acrimony at the end of the programme.

Clients usually ask several questions such as will they be under the hypnotist's total control, how long will the treatment take, will there be a relapse of the problem or any adverse affects following hypnosis, what will happen if they can not enter hypnosis, and so on. Most of these questions can be answered using the issues discussed in Chapter 1 in particular. Though some clients may be capable of entering hypnosis after a number of sessions, it may be impractical and counter-productive to continue attempting inducing hypnosis if it has not been achieved by the second or third session (See section on 'Resistance' in Chapter 3). Whether clients ask questions or not it is advisable to give adequate explanation.

## Preparation of the client

The two worries clients often express are whether they will lose all control to the hypnotist and do or say things they would regret, and the possible failure of entering hypnosis. The hypnotist must explain that the client will not be asked to say or do anything against his will and that in fact he can, even under hypnosis, refuse to do so; that if he encounters a moment when he finds himself revealing a confidence, it is most likely to be because he has enough trust in the hypnotherapist to do so, in the same way as he may, on an unexpected moment, open up to a friend. Indeed, some clients who might be attending for a course to give up smoking, may during a trance state decide to reveal personal details which may have nothing to do with their smoking problem, and which the hypnotist has not solicited.

Perhaps the most convincing argument is that most of the details related to any one session will be discussed with clients, for their approval, before any trance state is induced. Any deviation from the plan considered significant by the hypnotist will not be made and will be kept in abeyance for discussion after termination, and for the client's approval and possible subsequent use on another session. Alternatively, a client can be advised that if such changes or additions are considered essential, he will be asked whilst in the trance state whether he is agreeable to them.

Clients may wish to know in advance how they would recognise if they are experiencing a trance state. It should be explained that clients' accounts of such an experience vary considerably but that there are several signs which can not easily be faked and which a hypnotist looks out for. At this point, it would be unwise to describe these signs, as clients may, being pre-warned, manifest such signs volitionally. Clients should be assured that they will, after awakening, be given feedback on whether such signs were manifested.

Common trance experiences can be described to clients. They should be told that they are likely to feel very relaxed and perhaps even drowsy, that they will not be going to sleep (unless they are already very tired) and that they will be able to hear everything the hypnotist says - after all, if they can not, how are they going to be able to respond to the hypnotist's suggestions. They may also be able to hear environmental noises but these will be of no consequence to them as they will be concentrating on the hypnotist's voice. They will also be aware of the hypnotist's presence and may even be able to speak with him though, because they will be so relaxed, they may do so very slowly. The trance feeling has been likened to that state experienced when one is on the point of nodding off but not quite.

Reassurance must be given to clients that it does not really matter whether they enter a trance state on the first attempt, that not all subjects are hypnotisable, and so on. Consequently, they do not have to make any positive efforts to enter hypnosis nor respond to the hypnotist's suggestion just to please him. Not being able to enter a trance state is no personal failure for the hypnotist nor client. This needs to be said because some clients feel guilty if they feel they have not succeeded in experiencing hypnosis. It must also be explained that hypnotherapy may prove not to be the best strategy for their problem and that others may have to be considered.

Another worry that clients may express is not being able to wake up from the trance state. The chances of this happening are very negligible. However, the hypnotist should reassure clients that there are strategies available to overcome this unlikely problem, one of them being calling a fellow hypnotist to whom clients may more readily respond. It is thus, advisable for a hypnotherapist to know who to contact and how, in the event of this uncommon eventuality. Clients should be reassured that whilst the fellow hypnotist arrives, they will remain in the trance with no adverse effects.

Some hypnotherapists may feel that the less said, the better and that too much explanation may increase clients' anxiety. The amount and depth of explanation has to be gauged by the hypnotherapist's judgement as to its benefit, the client's affective state at the time and the hypnotherapist's evaluation of the client's capacity to understand such explanations.

Clients should also be reassured that confidentiality will be maintained at all times. They will be able to recall as much about their session as they normally would about any other wakeful experience. Popular misconceptions about hypnosis should be corrected, I would suggest, even if clients do not mention them as it is likely that they will have read about them in the popular press or even seen films giving them credit and may be too shy to raise them for discussion.

Finally, nothing can happen without a client's co-operation and this perhaps confirms that the hypotist is not all powerful. I like to tell clients that this is a collaborative exercise and that in the same way as a doctor can not help a patient if the latter does not follow instructions, I will not be able to help clients if they do not accept a partnership responsibility for their progress.

## Susceptibility tests

The phenomenon of 'susceptibility' has already been discussed in Chapter 1. The value of 'susceptibility' tests has been debated at length. It has been suggested that such tests may well be useful in experimental but not clinical work. There would seem to be little point in spending time finding out if a client is susceptible when all one needs to do is to attempt to induce a trance. If it is not successful, some argue, this means that the client is not susceptible. This is not quite true because the client may not be able to enter a trance for many reasons. Moreover, a client may fail to go into hypnosis in the first or even second session and may subsequently succeed.

A client may not respond to one hypnotist or induction technique, whilst responding to another. Susceptibility tests may or may not be valid, or reliable. Other factors such as the client's motivation and commitment may determine whether trance induction is possible, much more significantly than any measure of susceptibility. Some of the more common susceptibility tests however, are briefly described below. Many of these may well tap the level to which clients are willing to co-operate with the hypnotist and how well they can enter the necessary 'role'.

### *'Hand Clasp' Test*

A much used susceptibility test is the 'hand clasp' test. The client may be asked to clasp both hands, intertwining the fingers of one between the fingers of the other. The client is then asked to stretch both arms out in front (with or without eyes closed) and turn the hands palms outwards. In order to ensure that arms are kept stretched, the client may be asked to imagine that there is a red brick wall in front of him which would tumble down if not supported by the push of the hands. If necessary, the hypnotist can place his hand firmly against the client's, asking the latter to imagine the former's flattened hand to be the wall.

> "In a few moments' time, I shall remove my hand from yours but I want you to continue concentrating on pushing that 'wall' otherwise it will fall upon you. I am removing my hand now; keep on pushing hard. Now, on the count of three you are going to try and unclasp your hands whilst you keep on pushing that wall, but you will find it impossible/very difficult to do so."

If the client is co-operating, he will find it very difficult to unclasp his hands whilst his arms are extended fully - this is a physiological phenomenon.

Another variation of this requires the client to clasp his hands and rest them on his head whilst his arms hang heavily at the side of his face. Unclasping hands in this position is physiologically very difficult if not impossible.

### *The 'Orange' Test*

The success of the hand clasp test depends largely on the client's 'physical' co-operation. A test which depends on the client's imaginal ability is the 'orange' test. The hypnotist holds his hand high above his head and asks the client to imagine an orange being squeezed in the hypnotist's hand.

> "You can now see the orange being squeezed in my hand and soon you'll see the beautiful, golden juice being squeezed out and dripping down from my hand," etc.

Clients who have a good power of imagination will soon start salivating. One client, when asked what she was thinking about, when this test was being done, said "My main worry was that it was dripping down your shirt sleeve and was staining it!"

### 'Postural Sway' Test

This test is very often used. It is not only based on the effectiveness of the hypnotist's suggestion but also on the trust that a client has in the hypnotist. It is best to invite the client to remove his shoes, particularly if they have high heels. The client is asked to stand very straight and is directed to look at a spot above his head on the ceiling. The hypnotist stands behind the client with his hands on the client's shoulders and gently starts rocking the client backwards and forwards. As the client's balance is disturbed, the hypnotist instructs him to close his eyes but to continue looking upwards and imagine the spot on the ceiling.

"Maintain this standing position and just imagine you are becoming as stiff as a board .... your knees are stiff and your body is straight and rigid. As you continue looking upwards you will feel that an invisible force is pushing you backwards towards me .... making you lose your balance .... and making you feel that you are falling backwards. You do not need to resist this force because you will not fall to the ground as I am behind you to ensure this will not happen. You are now starting to fall backwards. You are falling .... falling .... falling ....."

As the client starts swaying, the suggestion is repeated and the hypnotist removes his hands from the client's shoulders. If the client actually starts falling backwards, the hypnotist is ready to prevent it. If the client tries to re-establish his balance, it is likely to be an indication that trust in the hypnotist has not been established.

### The 'Body Sway' Test

A variation of the postural sway test is the 'body sway' test. This test employs solely suggestion and the hypnotist does not touch the client nor initiate the sway. The hypnotist, whilst standing in front of the client, briefly explains the exercise to the client. A chair is strategically placed just behind the client who is asked to close his eyes and imagine a wind blowing against his back. Again, the hypnotist suggests that the client will start losing balance as the wind is getting stronger and stronger, pushing the client forwards. The hypnotist assures the client that if he starts falling forwards he will be caught, and if he starts falling backwards, the chair is behind to catch him. Rowley (1986) recommends that these suggestions need not be continued for more that two minutes by which time, if the client is not swaying, there is no point in continuing as any subsequent swaying behaviour is likely to be due to fatigue and not to susceptibility.

### 'Arm Heaviness/Levitation' Test

This test can either combine both suggestions of arm heaviness and levitation or just one of them. The client is asked to stretch both arms out forwards, one hand palm up and the other palm down. The hypnotist asks the client to imagine that a heavy weight is being held by the hand facing upwards and that whilst the other arm remains fairly still, the other one is descending as the weight makes it feel heavier and heavier. If arm levitation is being used, the client can be asked to imagine either that some invisible thread or force is pulling it up making it lighter and lighter or that it is being pushed upwards by some force from underneath. Arm levitation is a more effective test as the feeling of arm heaviness could be attributed to fatigue and the force of gravity.

The test could involve both arms accompanied by suitable suggestions. A positive response to this variation is perhaps more significant as the distance between each hand, when both are involved, will be greater and more dramatic. Hartland (1971) proposed a variation to the arm levitation test just described. The hypnotist places one hand on top of the client's whose arm rests, palm downwards, on a table. As the hypnotist lightly presses down on the client's hand, he suggests that it is getting lighter. If the client reports that his hand is not becoming lighter, the hypnotist relaxes the pressure and continues suggesting that the client's hand is now feeling increasingly lighter and soon it will start rising from the table and up into the air. The hypnotist gradually relaxes the pressure on the client's hand further as it starts rising, and eventually removes it entirely.

There are other subjective tests of susceptibility such as Chevreul's Pendulum Test, but the ones described above are perhaps the most common. One of the problems for the practitioner is in determining how a client's response to any one of these tests can be evaluated. There is no objective scale of measurement which will indicate how the client's behaviour during these tests can reflect a particular degree of susceptibility, a question, I hasten to add which many hypnotherapists feel has no clinical value except perhaps for convincing sceptical clients that their successful response indicates that they are in fact hypnotisable. The problem is that failure to respond to these tests as predicted, will equally as effectively strengthen the same clients' resolve that they are not hypnotisable.

### *'Objective' Susceptibility Tests*

Fellows (1988) states that objective tests of susceptibility are of more interest in experimental work but suggests that susceptibility scales can also give the hypnotherapist information about the amount of benefit a client might derive from hypnotherapy. Most of the work on objective susceptibility tests was conducted in the 50's by Weitzenhoffer and Hilgard (1959) who produced the Stanford Hypnotic Clinical Scale (SHCH) for children and another for adults was developed by Morgan and Hilgard (1978/79). Another scale, the Harvard Group Scale of Hypnotic Susceptibility (HGSHS), was devised for testing the susceptibility of groups of clients (Shor and Orne, 1962). Other tests are briefly reviewed by Fellows (op. cit.) and Rowley (op. cit.) and the reader is referred to these two publications for further elaboration.

The table on the folowing page provides a comparison and contrast of the items included in a selection of published susceptibility tests.

| TEST ITEMS | SHSS A & B | SHSS C | SHCS (children) | HGSHS | GAT | CIS |
|---|---|---|---|---|---|---|
| Postural Sway | | | | | | |
| Eye Closure | | | | | | |
| Limb-lowering | Hand | Hand | Hand | Lt. hand | | |
| - immobilisation | Arm | Arm | | Rt. Arm | | |
| - lock | Finger | | | Finger | | |
| - rigidity | Arm | Arm | Arm | Lt. Arm | | |
| - levitation | | | | | | Hand |
| - heaviness | | | | | | Arm |
| Hand moving | | | | | | |
| - together | ✓ | | | ✓ | | |
| - apart | | ✓ | | | | |
| Verbal Inhibition | ✓ | | | ✓ | ✓ | |
| Hallucinations | | | | | | |
| - Visual | ✓ | Negative | TV | | | Water |
| - Auditory | | Voice | TV | | | Music |
| - Olfactory | | | | | | ✓ |
| - Tactile | | Mosquito | | Fly | | |
| - Gustatory | | ✓ | | | | ✓ |
| - Temperature | | | | | | ✓ |
| Eye Catalepsy | ✓ | | | ✓ | | |
| Post-Hypnotic Suggestion | ✓ | | For older children | ✓ | ✓ | |
| Amnesia | ✓ | ✓ | | ✓ | ✓ | |
| Dream Induction | | ✓ | ✓ | | | |
| Age Regression | | ✓ | ✓ | | | |
| Anosmia (to ammonia) | ✓ | | | | | |
| Anaesthesia | | | | | | Finger |
| Head Falling | | | | ✓ | ✓ | |
| Alert Trance | | | | | ✓ | |
| Time Distortion | | | | | | ✓ |
| Mind-Body Relaxation | | | | | ✓ | |
| *Scoring* | 1 per item | 1 per item | 1 per item | *1 per item | *4 point scale | *5 point scale |
| *Time taken* | 45 mins | – | 20 mins | 1 hour | 45 mins | 25 mins |

*Self Administered/Scored

**KEY to abbreviations:** SHSS – Stanford Hypnosis Susceptibility Scale; SHCS – Stanford Hypnotic Clinical Scale for Children; HGSHS – Harvard Group Scale of Hypnotic Susceptibility; GAT – Group Alert Trance Scale; CIS – Creative Imagination Scale.

As can be seen from the table on the previous page, the tests vary in the amount of time they take to complete. There are several items common to most tests, mainly because some of these tests are versions of, or have been developed from, the SHSS. A quick analysis of the common items would provide the following list:

| Items in Susceptibility Tests | Number of Selected Tests including these items |
|---|---|
| Hallucination (of some form) | (5) |
| Hand lowering | (4) |
| Amnesia | (4) |
| Post Hypnotic Suggestion | (4) |
| Arm Rigidity | (4) |
| Arm Immobilisation | (3) |
| Age Regression | (3) |
| Verbal Inhibition | (3) |
| Hands moving together/apart | (3) |
| Eye Closure | (2) |
| Finger Lock | (2) |
| Hand/Arm Levitation | (2) |
| Eye Catalepsy | (2) |
| Head Falling | (2) |
| Dream Induction | (2) |

Interestingly, only one test includes Postural Sway. It seems to me that to achieve most of these items, a client would already have entered a trance state. It is possible, therefore, that positive responses to these items simply indicate susceptibility 'retrospectively' and not 'predictively'. These scales are therefore, more useful in indicating the extent of a client's trance-depth. Some scales are self-administered by the client and one wonders how objective this evaluation can be. On the other hand, this may not matter since it is the client's perception of the trance experience which is important.

## Final considerations

Before one makes the decision to use hypnosis, whether on its own or as an adjunct to another therapy, it is important that the information obtained during the interview is carefully evaluated. A cavalier decision to use hypnosis, particularly if the client has been referred for such treatment, or has self referred, may result in failure and subsequent frustration for both client and hypnotherapist. Such decisions made without a careful rationale could be construed as reflecting professional negligence. Hypnosis is not all powerful and sometimes one is encouraged to use it because everything else has failed.

The hypnotherapist should discuss with the client the nature of the therapy programme, listen to any comments the client makes, and address such issues or questions that the client raises. Unless the client feels that he understands what is likely to happen to him, at least in general terms, and what the therapist's intentions are, he is always likely to harbour some anxiety and fear which may detrimentally affect the success of the programme and reduce his motivation. The client should also be told that there will be ample opportunity before the session is over to discuss his reactions and feelings, and any outcome. He should also be told that before the session is over, new goals will be set for the next session.

## Conclusions

Hypnosis is usually one of the many therapeutic strategies in the health care professional's therapeutic armamentorium. As for any other therapy, the appropriateness for its use must be carefully rationalised after careful consideration of the presenting conditions, its suitability for the particular client and his circumstances. A well structured and unhurried interview with the client should be conducted prior to any decisions being made and a detailed case history taken. Information from other health care agencies should be considered, or requested, as appropriate.

Professional ethics demand that where the client's condition is known to be, or is suspected to possibly be medically related, the appropriate professional is consulted before hypnosis is attempted.

## CHAPTER 3
# Hypnosis – The Practice

## Samuel Abudarham

It is often said that hypnotic induction techniques do not normally take a trainee long to learn. This is probably generally true and may only require a demonstration and a 'script' suggesting a wording that can be used. It is therefore, not the technique which requires much training before it is mastered, but the rationale behind the selection of the most appropriate technique for any particular client. Before rushing into a decision to use hypnosis, a hypnotherapist must ensure that it is the most appropriate technique to employ not only with regards to the particular client but also regarding the condition to be treated (See Chapter 2). Careful consideration must therefore, be given to the outcome of a well conducted first interview. There are quite a variety of hypnotic induction techniques. The choice of any one technique largely depends on the client and, to some extent, the hypnotist. The former's personality, likely co-operation and the reason for the need for hypnotherapy may indicate the appropriateness of a particular technique. Experienced hypnotists very often feel more comfortable and have more faith in a small repertoire of techniques which they tend to use for most occasions. They should however, be 'au fait' with other techniques as not all clients respond well to any one technique. Several techniques will be briefly discussed following which the routine for a couple of my preferences will be considered.

Some hypnotic induction techniques are useful for inducing trances of mild depth. Others are more suitable when advanced depths are desirable; these are often referred to as simply 'deepening techniques'. In-built in some techniques, are suggestions that the client will achieve a trance at a later time or date, and usually in response to some sort of verbal command, or other stimulus, such as a touch or nod, usually executed by the therapist.

My experience when training students in hypnosis is that they often lay too much store and dependence on the routine script or 'patter'. Consequently, they often get distressed if they miss or misarticulate a word or phrase in the script. There is evidence that the importance attached to a prescribed form of wording has been overestimated. Very often, a client may be aware of a hypnotist's hesitation, self-correction, or even an ambiguous or incongruent message. Just as often, this does not make much difference and many clients tend to make their own adaptations as appropriate. This behaviour is not much different to adapting to what the listener knows a speaker is trying to say, without the former feeling the need to correct the latter.

There are of course times during a hypnosis session, especially during regression analysis and ego strengthening when the wording used must be precise. It sometimes happens that during the induction process, a hypnotist inadvertently over-directs the client when encouraging imaginary activities. Many clients often choose to disregard this direction and 'go their own way and at their own pace', particularly when they understand the objectives. However, some clients await the hypnotherapist's word, 'hand and foot' as it were, and will interpret the hypnotherapist's suggestions literally. With experience, the hypnotherapist learns a particular 'patter' and becomes less dependent on those forms suggested in text books. In induction techniques therefore, the rationale, objectives and principles of the particular technique may supersede the language used in importance. The validity of Neurolinguistic Programming resulting from induction techniques developed by Erickson, of which one objective is to find out and use language which clients find easiest to interpret, is queried by Heap (1988). Care should be taken, however, that the verbal routine is free of jargon and the language should be client appropriate.

It is probably true that any hypnotherapist can work quite effectively without the need to be proficient in many of the induction techniques discussed in the literature. Many practitioners soon learn to develop their own.

## Hypnotic induction techniques

The most frequently used categories of induction techniques is the one proposed by Hartland (1971). He suggested three major approaches: Permissive, Intermediate and Authoritarian techniques.

Permissive techniques involve making suggestions to the client in a non-authoritarian or over-directive manner. The client is persuaded that he shall be imagining certain things and that he will experience certain sensations or behaviours. Other than the suggestion sometimes considered necessary that the client can close his eyes, there is no other direct command and the client may be told that it is up to him whether he wishes to close his eyes or not. Because of their non-authoritarian nature, these techniques are probably more appropriate to clients who feel wary of, or threatened by, the experience of a trance state. Indications of this are usually given during the initial interview (See Chapter 2).

Authoritarian techniques are more directive. During these techniques the hypnotist will issue suggestions in the form of orders 'you will'. The hypnotist presents such orders in a domineering and assertive fashion. These techniques are suitable for some clients who clearly expect to be told what to do. Again, indications of this can be obtained during the first interview. There are, however, three main disadvantages of such an approach. If a client is worried about losing all control to the hypnotist, he may resist being directed. Clients who are over-analytic, sceptical or critical about hypnosis or the nature of the induction technique, or who critically monitor their responses to the 'orders', may decide to resist and sometimes even do the opposite of what the hypnotist tells them, often just to assert their own independence. The second disadvantage is that success depends on whether and how quickly the order is actually carried out. There is a limit to the number of times one can repeat that something is going to happen without the order losing its impact. The third disadvantage may be in a conflict between a particular suggestion by the hypnotist and clients' reluctance to respond for fear of the consequence or because they do not wish to reveal a private matter. Furthermore, if the order is not carried out, the client is likely to lose confidence in the hypnotist.

A useful technique of the authoritarian type which is particularly appropriate for clients who may find it difficult to keep their eyes closed was developed as a modification of a technique first employed by Elman (1964). The client is asked to close his eyes and encouraged to progressively relax from head to toe. Special attention is given to achieving a degree of relaxation of the eyes to a point when it would be difficult to open them on suggestion. However, the client is then instructed to open his eyes and that on closing them again he will feel doubly as relaxed. The routine is repeated with instructions that every time he opens and closes his eyes the level of relaxation will get deeper.

## Erickson's 'Confusional Technique'

Erickson's 'Confusional Technique' is not easy to use and requires particular training for the hypnotist. The aim is to provoke a state in a client when he is unsure as to whether he is co-operating or not. The induction routine requires expert use of verbal messages to the client which are either ambiguous, seemingly incongruent or conflicting. This serves to confuse the client who eventually develops a need for clear instructions from the hypnotist. The technique has been found useful for clients who may express the wish to be hypnotised but subconsciously resist any attempts by a hypnotist to do so.

## Intermediate Techniques

Intermediate techniques may employ a combination of a permissive and authoritarian techniques. For example, a client is directed to do something and at the same time suggestions are made by the hypnotist that the client may feel more relaxed and may wish to close his eyes. An example of this is the 'Eye Fixation with Distraction' technique briefly described below (See 'Combined Techniques').

Another Intermediate technique is the 'Hand Levitation Method' proposed by Erickson. The hypnotist instructs the client to sit and stare at his own hands which are spread out palm downwards on his lap. The hypnotist then directs the client to sensations he can feel in his hands; firstly, slight muscular movements which then develop into the fingers spreading and gradually a feeling that the fingers and hands are getting lighter until they actually start rising into the air in the direction of the face. As soon as the hand touches a part of the face, e.g. the nose, the hypnotist suggests, the client will feel deeply relaxed and his eyes will feel heavier and heavier until they close. The arm will then drop on the client's lap or by the side. Whereas a slight variation of this method is very effective as a deepening technique it is not as effective as an induction technique (See section on "Deepening Techniques" below).

## *Eye-Fixation Techniques*

Perhaps the most commonly used induction techniques involve eye-fixation accompanied by suggestions of relaxation, and so on, by the hypnotist. The client is told to fix his gaze on a particular stimulus such as a spot on the ceiling above and somewhat behind his head, his own thumb nail whilst holding his hand up above his head, or even on the hypnotist's index and third finger held in a V-sign (a colleague affectionately calls this the 'Churchill' technique) two feet or so above the client at a point where the client can only see them by rolling his eyes as far up as possible. A variation to the thumb nail technique requires the client to gaze at the nail of his own thumb held in an upright position in front of his eyes and at arm's length. The client is asked to very slowly rotate his thumb and that when it reaches a downwards point his eyes will want to close.

Other techniques of eye-fixation may require a client to observe the tip of a pen placed about six inches above the eyes, or to follow with their eyes an item being brought up and down in front of the client's eyes without movement of the head. Two eye-fixation methods popularised by the cinema are the 'eye-to-eye fixation gaze' requiring the client to gaze into the hypnotist's eyes. The hypnotist should not wear spectacles for this method and should also make sure that he keeps moving his own eyes or risk entering a trance himself!

Another one is often referred to as 'Chevreul's Pendulum' technique. The client sits face kept forward and the hypnotist dangles a pendulum from a string about 12 inches long approximately six inches above the client's eye level. The client is required to follow the sway of the pendulum whilst the hypnotist goes through an induction technique. Somehow, I have never been too enamoured with these two techniques perhaps because they smack too much of stage hypnotism, though I have on occasions employed them.

The eye-fixation approach was initially employed by Braid who thought that the eye-fixation itself induced hypnosis. This is now known not to be the case. One disadvantage of this method is that it sometimes encourages some clients to concentrate on the visual stimulus to such an extent that the exercise takes over in importance and they make strenuous efforts to keep their eyes open. More commonly however, eye-fixation techniques place a strain on the eyes and one can predict that sooner or later the normal physiological response of blinking and ultimately the wish to rest the eyes will occur. The hypnotist can thus, tell the client in advance that soon his eyes will start blinking and he may eventually wish to close his eyes. As the blinking starts, the hypnotist can call attention to the behaviour and so reinforce these suggestions. The client may thus, gain confidence that subsequent suggestions will equally come true.

## *Combined Techniques*

Eye-fixation is often combined with other strategies such as a distraction exercise or progressive relaxation. In the former, the client is asked to go through a mental exercise designed to distract him from the hypnotist's induction routine such as counting up to or down from 300. He is told that it is not really important to count accurately and that he may reach a point when he will make errors. If this happens, he is to proceed regardless to the next number and not revise any errors. He is also prewarned that at some point he will stop counting and may indeed not have got anywhere near 300. He must not be concerned about this because what is more important is that as he counts he will be listening to everything the therapist will be saying to him.

When eye-fixation is combined with progressive-relaxation, the client is asked to fix their gaze on a visual stimulus and allow relaxation to spread from feet up throughout each part of the body. My preference is to wait until the client's eyes close and then encourage relaxation from the eyes, spreading down the face, jaws, neck, shoulders, arms and so on. The reason for this is that the feeling of relaxation is best perceived by contrast with tension and since the eyes have been straining for a while before closing, as soon as the eyelids close the tension felt in the eyes starts reducing. One can thus, reinforce this feeling by calling the client's conscious attention to this (physiological) reaction (see Appendix for 'Induction Routine').

### Relaxation Techniques

There are many techniques which do not employ eye-fixation. A common one uses progressive relaxation through verbal suggestion alone. Others may make use of a client's powers of imagination. He may be asked to close his eyes and imagine himself in a very peaceful and relaxing environment - the countryside, beach or holiday spot may be suitable scenes. The initial interview usually suggests a client's favourite situation and which he finds relaxing. Equally so, the hypnotist can find out which situations provoke tension in clients and steer clear of those. One client I had, hated the beach because he could not stand the sun or heat. As a contrast, and perhaps the most memorable client I have had in this respect, was an Israeli ex-paratrooper who found the descent by parachute a very relaxing experience. This approach was particularly useful because we were able to identify a beginning of the relaxation process and a stage to aim for, which when reached, the client would feel totally relaxed. I do not think many clients would relish this scenario, imaginary or otherwise.

### Active Techniques

There are other techniques sometimes employed with children which can also be successfully used with adults which require more complicated activity by the client. Among these are the 'Television', the 'Blackboard' and the 'Beach Ball' techniques. These are sometimes referred to as 'Active Techniques'. They are described briefly below under the heading of "Hypnosis with Children".

## Overcoming resistance

Some clients, though expressing their commitment to a course of hypnotherapy, and even after explanations and assurances by the hypnotist, may still be resistant to entering a trance state. On occasions, clients may resist suggestions of closing their eyes. Eye closure is not in fact crucial so an induction routine not requiring initial eye closure such as Erickson's Hand Levitation Method (see above) can be employed. Once levitation starts and the hypnotist starts suggesting that the client will start feeling more relaxed and drowsier as his hand and arm rise higher and higher, further suggestions can be made, if necessary, that the client's eyes will feel heavier and will eventually close.

Another technique requires the client to open and close his eyes perhaps whilst fixing his gaze on a spot on the ceiling. Suggestions are made that as he does this, and if he wishes to relax, his eyes will get heavier and heavier until at some point he will not open them again and will just relax.

Some clients may become a little confused or worried if they experience a cataleptic eye flutter, or they may find it difficult to determine when to allow their eyes to close. If this happens, the hypnotist can reassure them by saying "it is alright for you to allow your eyes to close now." If some hesitancy is still exhibited, the hypnotist can give a direct command, in a firm or gentle tone of voice, "I am going to count down from 3 and then say the word *NOW*. When I do so, you will close your eyes."

Perhaps the best approach to overcoming eye closure prior to induction, is to ask the client to close his eyes and just relax as he would when on his own or just before going to sleep. The hypnotist should reassure such a client that no attempt will be made to induce a trance. After a minute or so, the client is then told to open his eyes and asked if he felt reasonably relaxed. If he answers in the affirmative, it can then be pointed out to him that the trance experience is similar except he will feel much more relaxed.

## Signs of trance

Recognising when a client has achieved a trance state is not always easy particularly when it is a mild one. There are several signs however, which may be present and indicative of the client entering, or that he has indeed entered a trance state. The one I usually look out for is the 'cataleptic eye flutter' which is characterised by a rapid quiver of the eyelids just before the client closes his eyes. However, this is not always present and its absence does not imply that a client is not entering or has not entered a trance. When it does occur, it is usually a sign that the client is either on the threshold of hypnosis or, it may sometimes indicate that the depth of trance is increasing rather than decreasing.

Another sign of hypnosis may be the movement, often upwards, of the eyeballs under closed eyelids. Other forms of catalepsy may also indicate that a client has entered a trance state. A common type is the rigid catalepsy resulting in the client being able to maintain a rigid limb in a raised posture for a longer period of time than one would expect to be possible by voluntary effort alone. Suggestions that the arm is so rigid that any amount of effort on the client's part to flex it would be abortive, can be validated by following such suggestions with an invitation to the client to try to flex the arm. Often the arm is so rigid that one can clearly observe the client's strenuous efforts to bend it, to no avail.

Another sign involving a limb is the phenomenon sometimes referred to as 'levitation'. A hypnotist can suggest to the client in a trance that his arm (or even leg) will feel lighter and eventually rise up into the air without any effort on his part. Further mention of these phenomena, especially in relation to their use in deepening techniques, will be made later on in this chapter. The signs of a trance state mentioned above involve voluntary muscles behaviour and these are the most observable.

The client may manifest deep relaxation sometimes characterised by very limp limbs, lack of facial expression and, either slow speech, or long pauses between phrases, or between the hypnotist's question and the client's answers. Some clients relax so well that they tend to swallow excessively. Whereas muscle relaxation may also be indicative of hypnosis, such relaxation can be achieved by some clients without necessarily experiencing a trance state. Another observable sign may manifest itself in a change of skin pallor. Perhaps the sign one expects to always witness is a change in respiratory rate. As the client relaxes, the rate may slow down and respiration becomes shallower. On occasions, as clients relax further, they may produce a deep sigh at different stages.

Other signs of a trance state are indicated by a client's ability to experience changes in visual, tactile, auditory, olfactory and gustatory sensation, following suggestion from the hypnotist. An example of one of these is paraesthesia, for example numbness, increased sensitivity to pressure or pain, anaesthesia, i.e. loss of sensation (though maintaining other sensations such as pressure) sometimes within a 'marked' area of the body, and analgesia, i.e. pain reduction or removal.

Whether a client has achieved a trance state or not is perhaps not as important as whether he believes he has; in fact, on some occasions, my own conclusions in this respect and the client's perception have not always matched. If the client believes he has achieved hypnosis, it may not really matter very much whether the hypnotherapist concurs or not. It is when the opposite happens and the hypnotist feels that the client has entered into hypnosis and the client disagrees that may be more therapeutically counterproductive.

## Evaluating speed and depth of trance

In most cases, only a light or medium trance needs to be induced for hypnotherapy to be effective. I have found the distraction technique requiring the client to count as the induction is taking place, very useful in determining the speed in which a trance has been established and sometimes the subsequent depth achieved. An average client loses count after forward counting to up to 70 though many of the more hypnotisable clients report not getting beyond a count of twenty.

Again, it is usually only after the client is brought out of hypnosis and asked how deep he felt he had gone that one can obtain some sort of idea. To my knowledge, there is no objective and reliable way of determining the exact nature of the phenomena and I am not sure that it is of much clinical significance as the client's perception is more relevant. The wish to be able to do so is often more related to the underconfidence and ego of the hypnotist. It is true, however, that clients often express disappointment if they feel they have not experienced hypnosis. With many of these clients, attempts by the hypnotist to convince them to the contrary are likely to change their minds.

Several authorities discuss indicators of different trance depth; Waxman (1989) describes five levels, namely, hypnoidal, light, medium, deep and somnambulistic stages. They suggest that once a subject closes his eyes he enters "the threshold of the hypnotic state ...." which can be considered " .... a hypnoidal state which will imperceptibly drift into the light state of hypnosis". They believe that present day E.E.G. instruments can not differentiate between the wake state and the light stage. There is no objective way of identifying the point at which one stage develops into a deeper stage and any classification is "arbitrarily made for the convenience of therapy". Ninety per cent of the population can achieve a light trance.

When a client enters a medium stage, his respiration rate slows down and he responds to simple suggestions by the hypnotist. The client can be asked to signal, through raising his index finger perhaps, whether he is experiencing images and altered sensations. Whereas some degree of analgesia is possible, amnesia cannot be achieved during this stage and the client remains aware of everything including environmental stimuli. Seventy per cent of the general public can achieve this state. Only 20 per cent of these subjects can enter a deeper stage. Those who do may show it by a more relaxed facial expression, reduced respiration rate and flaccidity of the limbs - this last one can easily be confirmed by the hypnotist by gently raising the client's arm from the wrist and letting it drop back to its previous or other point of rest. At this stage amnesia, arm catalepsy, considerable degrees of analgesia and post-hypnotic suggestion can be achieved.

Only five per cent of hypnotisable subjects can achieve a somnambulistic stage. Whereas the client remains under hypnosis, he is usually able to behave as if awake, walk about the room with eyes open, talk and still respond to the hypnotist's instructions.

These figures have little practical value for the hypnotherapist as it is not possible to predict which category or "percentage" a client falls into until the particular depth has been achieved. Furthermore, clients entering a light stage in early sessions may achieve a deeper one in subsequent sessions. Many clients, with the right deepening techniques, can in fact be trained, over a period of time, to achieve greater trance depths. The figures given above may in fact not be reflected in one's case load. In my experience, a client's depth may vacillate within one trance period, thus preventing any firm decision of the depth achieved from being made. This observation is not insignificant as some clients often report some uncertainty about having experienced a trance state because they have had varying sensations of different states of altered awareness. This fact makes any self-report scales such as the Extended North Carolina Scale unreliable.

## Triggers and ideomotor responses (IMR)

A 'trigger' may be a stimulus of any kind, usually auditory (e.g. word), visual (e.g. a nod by the hypnotist), or tactile (e.g. touching the client's hand or back of the neck) that a hypnotist would use in order to get a desired response from the client. It often signals to the client when a predetermined response is expected. For example, a client may be told that after a count of say, five, the hypnotist will say the word *NOW* and on hearing this word the client will feel twice as relaxed as before. Another example is the word *PAST* in regression analysis when on response to that word a client will regress to an earlier age. Trigger stimuli are very useful as long or complex commands do not need to be repeated unduly once the client is told what form of behaviour(s) is associated with a particular trigger. The trigger can also be employed post-hypnotically when under hypnosis the client is told that a little while after waking up or perhaps on the next encounter, a trance will return in response to a trigger. Exphasising and drawing out verbal triggers in a firm but relaxed manner is thought to help clients respond.

The ideomotor response (IMR), or ideomotor finger-signalling technique, is one used to facilitate a client's response to questions asked by the hypnotist. Once the client is in hypnosis, the hypnotist explains that a link will be established between the client's sub-conscious mind and the index finger of one hand. The hypnotist starts by suggesting to the client that this finger is soon going to feel lighter, without any voluntary effort on the client's part, and as it does so, it will rise slowly but surely into the air. At first, the hypnotist suggests, the client may feel small twitches of the muscles of that finger. If any twitching is in fact observed, the hypnotist reinforces this response by calling the client's attention to it and suggesting that the finger will soon be ready to rise (see Appendix for 'IMR Routine').

On occasions, it may be necessary to heighten the client's awareness of the relevant finger, by gently stroking it and saying 'this finger'. Once the finger rises, even a small distance from where it is resting (usually on the client's lap if sitting down or from the abdomen if lying down), the hypnotist proceeds by suggesting that everything is now ready for this response to be linked with the sub-conscious mind. A trigger word such as *NOW* can be employed to signal the start of this link. It could be that the IMR is linked to affirmative answers given by the client.

It is often useful to suggest to the client that the IMR will now respond when the hypnotist says the word *YES*. The hypnotist then proceeds to do this. The IMR may be a little delayed but when it happens, the hypnotist reinforces it by complimenting the client and suggesting that the finger can return to its resting position. Sometimes the finger does not go down, so the hypnotist can gently push it down. The exercise is repeated a few times until the IMR is well established in response to the trigger word. Further testing of this can be done by saying to the client that if the response to a few simple questions asked is in the affirmative, the IMR will indicate this. The hypnotist can then ask a selection of questions to which affirmative and negative answers will be given by the client - information from the interview will indicate in which way the questions should be answered. The hypnotist then suggests that any time the "non-conscious" mind wishes to give an affirmative answer, it will indicate this by the IMR. Once satisfied about the reliability of the IMR response, it can be used during the hypnoanalysis or hypnotherapy part of a programme. The IMR is particularly useful in regression analysis.

Care must be taken before starting to establish the IMR, that all the client's fingers are free to move, particularly since sometimes it is not the 'nominated' finger which responds but another: clients should not be encouraged to clasp their hands as this restricts finger movement, the best hand position being flat on the client's abdomen (if lying down) or lap (if sitting). The client's finger should also be clearly visible to the hypnotist as sometimes the IMR is very slight though indicative nonetheless.

Some hypnotherapists establish an IMR on the index fingers of both hands for opposing answers; for example, the right index finger for 'affirmative' and the left for 'negative'. This is sometimes done because the absence of an IMR using one finger alone does not always indicate a negative response to a question. Establishing an IMR in both hands therefore, makes the response less equivocal. A modification to this involves the establishment of an IMR on another finger to indicate the client's wish not to answer or a 'don't know' response. Some clients find the use of more than one finger to differentiate between the different responses confusing and may thus, not be able to respond reliably.

It is in fact not necessary for the hypnotist to prescribe which finger should rise. It can be suggested to the client that any one of the fingers will rise to an affirmative thought or response, a different finger will rise to a negative thought or response, etc.. So long as the finger raised consistently accords with a particular answer, the exercise can be just as reliable.

Both 'triggers' and IMRs should be 'extinguished' before the client is brought out of hypnosis and if it is not going to be used again in that session. This is simply done through suggestion that

> "no longer are you going to respond to the triggers that I have used, such as (e.g the word NOW) and the link between your subconscious mind and your finger will be broken as soon as you come out of hypnosis."

A post hypnotic suggestion for the use of triggers or IMRs in future sessions can be made so that one does not need to spend time unnecessarily in repeating the whole routine from the beginning. If necessary, at the next session, and once the client goes into hypnosis, he can be reminded of the triggers and told that he will respond with the IMR as he did in the previous session.

## Handling a client's self-induced hyperventilation

On very few occasions, a client may experience a self-induced momentary episode of hyperventilation. The client will be seen to be taking unduly deep, continuous, and sometimes irregular inhalations. It has to be stressed that this happens very rarely but if the hyperventilation is excessive and were to last long enough, there could be a danger of tetany due to oxygen intoxication. In order to avoid this, an appropriate response by the hypnotherapist is to suggest strongly to the client that "... you are now beginning to feel more ... and more relaxed ... your breathing is becoming easier ... and easier ... shallower ... relaxed," etc..

Once a more regular breathing pattern has been restored, the client should be asked how he feels. Having established that the client is calm and in control, the client can be asked if there were any thoughts or feelings just prior to and during the hyperventilating episode which may have caused it. Another strategy is to ask the client to breathe into a paper bag placed tightly round the mouth. With every inhalation, there will be an amount of the carbon dioxide breathed out during the previous exhalation which will thus reduce the amount of oxygen taken in on inhalation. As the client is doing this, suggestions of calm and relaxation are continuously made until the client responds accordingly. Under hypnosis, some clients may find it difficult to follow the instruction "... breathe into a paper bag ..."

They may respond more readily if they are instructed to imagine that they are "... blowing up a balloon which will make your breathing easier..." and they do so imagining the paper bag to be a balloon.

Most of these very rare occurrences can be effectively dealt with using the first of these methods. If however, the hypnotherapist has cause for concern, the client should be asked to relax and asked if he wishes to be brought out of hypnosis. If the client does not reply, the hypnotherapist should then consider gently bringing the client out of hypnosis. Of course, if the hyperventilation has occurred when the client has been regressed (see below) then he should be brought back to his actual age before termination. Reassuring words such as "in a few moments ...... I shall be counting down from five ..... and when I finish counting .... I shall say the word *NOW*. When I say the word ... *NOW* ..... you will open your eyes ..... and you will find yourself ... back in my (consulting) room ... feeling quite relaxed ..... and secure ... calm ... and refreshed" etc..

When out of hypnosis, the client can be invited to discuss his experience and whenever necessary, appropriate explanation and reassurance should be given.

## Reluctance to come out of hypnosis

A small number of clients may exhibit reluctance to come out of hypnosis. Before one takes any further action, one needs to ensure that the client has indeed not fallen asleep. In one case, a client of mine attended a session after an extremely tiring day. He seemed very relaxed moments after the induction was commenced. Suspecting that he had perhaps not gone into hypnosis, I decided to bring him out in the usual manner (see 'Termination' below) but he did not respond. Just as I was going to persevere in my termination routine, my growing suspicions were vindicated by the client beginning to snore! In such cases, a client can be awoken by calling his name out and asking him to wake up, perhaps with the aid of a gentle shaking of his arm.

On occasions, a client has misinterpreted the suggestion to come out of hypnosis. A client's reluctance to come out of a trance could also be due to a wish not to comply with a post-hypnotic suggestion. If this is a possibility, the client should be asked, and if confirmed, the post-hypnctic suggestion should be withdrawn.

Many clients enjoy the trance experience and find it very relaxing, to the extent that they are reluctant to be brought out of hypnosis. Sometimes this reluctance is also determined by a wish not to be brought back to a reality they do not wish to face again. On occasions, this response may underlie a conversion symptom so that remaining in a relaxed, hypnctic trance no longer necessitates facing further problems. In this case, the client should be given appropriate reassurance.

Several other strategies may be employed. The client can be asked directly what needs to be done to terminate the trance and often, the client will oblige with a suggestion. Another approach is to use a routine to deepen the trance and then use the usual strategy to terminate. Yet another approach which is not always feasible is to introduce another hypnotherapist to the client who will take over and attempt to terminate the trance.

Recently, I had an interesting experience of a client who had been reluctant to enter hypnosis. She knew why but would not say. After a few sessions during which her wishes were respected, she developed a healthy trust in me and declared that she was now ready to allow herself to be hypnotised. During a session when she had been regressed to an earlier age, she suddenly started showing some signs of distress. She started crying and I asked her whether she wanted to come out of hypnosis. She rejected the suggestion saying that she knew she had to resolve her problem and that she had gone this far, and no matter how painful it was, she did not want to postpone the experience to another date. It turned out that she subconsciously knew that her problems went back to her childhood. She had been a constant victim of sexual abuse by her father. It was not until she developed sufficient confidence and trust in me that she had felt able to investigate through recall under hypnosis, her traumatic past. When she came out of hypnosis, she described her experience as a terrible nightmare which she had always felt she had to one day go through. She reported that she did not regret one moment of it as she then felt that a heavy emotional load had been lifted off her. Hypnotherapy and hypnoanalysis had helped her face a traumatic past which she felt was entirely responsible for the problem she had sought help for.

## Hypnosis with children

It is generally agreed that it is easier to hypnotise children than adults. This may perhaps be because given the right rapport between hypnotist and child, the latter enters more easily into a trusting relationship. Some of the induction techniques already discussed in this Chapter may not be suitable for children.

The earliest age at which a child can be induced into a hypnotic trance is generally agreed to be seven though much depends on factors other than age. There are many skills an individual needs to have before hypnotic induction can be successful. Younger children may not have developed the linguistic and cognitive skills required. They may find it difficult to attend and co-operate with the hypnotist. They might be distracted from the task in hand constantly and they may not be able to channelise their imagination as might be required. Once a child acquires these skills, certain induction techniques can successfully be employed. I have been able to successfully and effectively induce trances in children as young as six, and Kroger (1977) suggests that even some five year olds can be hypnotised.

What is very important is that the child is prepared well for the routine. It should be explained to him that he is going to be invited to play a game with the hypnotist but he needs to listen carefully otherwise he will not be able to learn it. He is told that at some point the hypnotist is going to ask him to pretend to go to sleep. (Some hypnotists will only use the term 'sleep' with children). The most effective induction techniques are those which best capture the child's imagination. Some of these techniques are the 'active' type.

### The 'Beachball' Technique

The child is asked to imagine that he has a beachball. He is instructed to close his eyes and to visualise the size, shape and colour of the beachball. The hypnotist can ask the child to describe the ball to him and if necessary help him with the description. All this has to be done showing enthusiasm and complimenting the child on his efforts. The 'story' can then be continued something like this

".... In a few moments time we are going to try and bounce that ball as high as we can. Now you know how difficult it is to bounce a beachball and so we have to try extra hard. I am going to help you at the beginning by holding your hand to bounce the ball up and down. So I am now reaching out for your hand .... and there (placing his hand on child's, both in a palm down position). Are you ready now .... let's start bouncing the ball together.... on the count of three .... ready .... one, two and.... three. Right. Let's bounce ...."

The hypnotist then pushes the child's hand down a few inches "let's count the bounces and see how many we can do .... ONE" and then helps him raise his hand by a few inches. As the counting goes on, the hypnotist urges the child to bounce the ball "higher and higher and down, .... 2 .... that's good .... it's really going high now ..." etc.

"Gosh – isn't this tiring work but we must get that ball to bounce even higher ... and soon you'll start getting more and more tired as we bounce the ball higher and even higher. Now, you keep your eyes on that ball. And soon you'll start getting so tired that you will start feeling very, very sleepy ...."

At an appropriate time, as the child is showing signs of tiredness, the hypnotist tells him

"You are doing so .... well, that I think you can carry on bouncing the ball all on your own .... so you .... carry on .... all on your own .... bounce the ball higher and higher ...."

The child is urged to continue moving his arm up and down as he imagines the bouncing. Invariably, the child soon gets so tired that he stops 'bouncing' though as soon as the hypnotist observes the child entering a trance, he can suggest that he has done so very well and that now that he's feeling so tired and sleepy, he can stop bouncing the ball.

### The 'Blackboard' Technique

There are several variations of this technique though they all require the child (or adult) to imagine he is standing at a blackboard. One approach is to ask the client to imagine he has a chalk in his hand. He is urged to physically stretch his arm out to "write" the number "1" on the blackboard and then erase it. Then number "2" which is erased as well. This carries on and at an appropriate time suggestions of tiredness or relaxation are made by the therapist. Obviously, this approach is only appropriate for children who can write numbers.

### The 'T.V.' or 'Picture Visualisation' Technique

Before employing this technique, it would help the hypnotist to be 'au fait' with children's television programmes and/or stories. The child is asked what his favourite programme is. He is then invited to close his eyes and pretend that he is sitting in front of his television. He is urged to turn it on, only to see his favourite programme is on, except that the picture is a bit fuzzy. To make it clearer, the child is told, or is helped, to slowly raise his hand from his lap and as it does so the picture becomes clearer and clearer. The hypnotist suggests that as the picture becomes clearer so the child can get more interested in the programme and as the child's hand goes higher and higher, he is feeling more and more tired. Depending on the hypnotist's ability to describe the scene, he can often enhance the scenario with suggestions such as when the child touches his nose he is going to hear his favourite music. The moment he hears the music, he can start conducting it with the index finger of one hand. He therefore, has to listen to the music carefully in order to be able to conduct it well.

Other techniques such as eye-fixation with progressive relaxation or counting may also be effective with older children.

## Ethical considerations with the young client

I always insist that parents or guardians remain in the room when hypnotising children. It is also very important to obtain their consent (written, preferably) to the use of hypnotherapy with their child. Once it is decided that hypnotherapy is likely to help, the phenomenon, procedures and aims must be explained to the parents and they should be invited to ask questions, in the same way as if they were the clients. On occasions, children will find it hard to co-operate with parents present and the more extroverted ones will "play to the audience" and not co-operate as required, even pretending that they have entered a trance. If the hypnotist suspects this is happening, the parents can be asked to leave the room and if the induction is successful, and if not contraindicated, invited back once the child is in hypnosis and before any hypnotherapy is commenced. Witnessing such a session may help parents to develop insights into the child's problem and the remediation techniques used. It also assures parents of the hypnotist's professional conduct.

## Deepening techniques

As has been stated earlier, effective therapy is possible with a mild trance. However, on occasions a deeper trance is desirable.

There are many published deepening techniques but these must never be employed in an 'off the peg' type of way without consideration of the particular client's personality, affective state and problem. Information from the interview can be useful criteria for the selection of a deepening technique. For example, it can be very distressing for clients allergic to pollen if a deepening routine requires them to imagine themselves descending into a garden. Similarly, asking a client with a fear of heights to imagine himself parachuting down from an aeroplane (see example given earlier on) may result in the client getting unnecessarily distressed. It is therefore, prudent to ask clients what situations they find relaxing and consider these for use in deepening routines. Most deepening routines require clients to use their imaginative skills. For those who are not able to do so, a more authoritarian approach may be indicated.

### *Active Techniques*

#### *Arm Levitation*

This is a popular deepening technique. Once the client has entered a mild trance state, the hypnotist suggests that he imagine himself in a very relaxing atmosphere, perhaps of his own choice. He may be with friends or members of the family one of whom approaches with a helium (light gas) filled balloon tied at the end of a string. This person then playfully ties the string round the client's wrist. On a trigger word by the hypnotist, this person will have finished tying the balloon and will be letting it go up into the air. Because the client's arm is so relaxed it offers no resistance to the balloon which, with an initial tug, continues its ascent into the sky, slowly and surely pulling the wrist up and raising the hand from the client's lap. As the hand or wrist shows some sign of movement, the hypnotist reinforces the behaviour by calling it to the client's attention and suggests that soon "the whole arm from shoulder to fingers will rise from the lap higher and higher." As it does so, the client "will feel more and more relaxed, going deeper and deeper into relaxation, with every upward movement of the arm."

The arm will be seen to 'jerk' its way up if the client is indeed in a trance. If the arm leaves the client's lap smartly and rises smoothly and/or quickly, the chances are that the client is using voluntary effort to achieve this behaviour and is unlikely to be in hypnosis. It sometimes helps if the client's attention is distracted from the hand/arm by asking him to concentrate carefully on the appearance of the balloon as he imagines it, whilst the hypnotist continues suggestions about further levitation and increasing trance depth. The hypnotist should also suggest a direction for the arm movement and a target, for example, the client's nose or if the arm is not rising high enough, the hypnotist can place his hand a little distance above the client's. The hypnotist then suggests that the moment the client's hand touches the predetermined point (the client's nose or hypnotist's hand), the client is going to feel doubly as relaxed.

This technique has the advantage that the experience of arm levitation provides for the client a very concrete and often dramatic sign of a response to the hypnotist in whom confidence is increased. Other imagery can be employed such as suggesting to the client that he concentrates on an imaginary spot on the back of one hand which is resting palm down on his lap. A piece of string is attached to this spot and an invisible force then pulls the string, raising the hand which already feels very light etc..

On occasions, some clients do not respond to arm levitation and they are so relaxed that they find the idea of a 'relaxed, heavy' hand becoming 'light', incongruous. Such clients can at times be helped by the hypnotist lifting their hand by the wrist ("In a few moments, I am going to give your hand a little help by lifting it from your lap to show you how relaxed it is, etc. .... I am now going to reach out for your wrist, etc."). The client's hand will often remain in that position (about three inches from the lap) when the hypnotist lets go of it, and on further suggestion will levitate further.

*Arm Rigidity*

Further deepening can be associated with suggestions that after the client's hand touches the predetermined point, it will then start stretching out in front of him. The client is then asked to imagine that the arm is becoming as stiff as a rod of iron, and will extend from shoulder to finger tips. As it does so, so the client will feel more and more relaxed. The stiffness can be demonstrated by suggesting to the client that he will be able to maintain that position for longer than he would have been able to when awake and without any effort. In fact, the arm can become so rigid that any attempt to push it down by the hypnotist or to flex it by the client will meet with effortless resistance. "In a few moments now you are going to want to bend your arm at the elbow but you will find this extremely difficult .... in fact the more you try to bend, the stiffer it will become and you will go deeper and deeper into hypnosis," etc..

In cases where arm levitation has not succeeded or has been contraindicated, a more authoritarian approach to arm rigidity might be required. The hypnotist can then lift the whole arm and hand from the client's lap, gently stretching it out whilst suggesting that soon the arm will become very rigid and as it does so, relaxation will become deeper.

As soon as the desired objective is achieved, the client can be instructed that following a trigger word or other stimulus, the arm, hand and fingers will recover their natural feeling and position and still very relaxed will start becoming heavier and land on the client's lap. "As it does so," suggests the hypnotist, "relaxation will become even deeper."

*Non-Active Visualisation Techniques*

Depth can similarly be achieved, by asking the client to imagine himself, at the top of a flight of steps leading to an exotic garden. As the client takes each of a predetermined number of steps down, so relaxation will increase until at last on arrival into the garden, relaxation will double. A similar scenario can be suggested with the client entering an 'Aladdin's cave' and getting more relaxed as he approaches a particularly beautiful and valuable object for closer inspection.

There is in fact no end of imaginative scenarios which can be used depending on the client's predilections. The hypnotist can choose the detail with which a situation is described for the client but my preference is to allow the client to imagine the detail of his own choice, with only some vague suggestions on *my* part. ("It is as warm as you usually like .... observe the beautiful colours of those flowers ..." as opposed to "It's nice and *hot* ... observe the *fuschias* and *daffodils* ..."). One I have often found useful is asking the client to imagine a peaceful scene on the beach. As the client stares out into the sea, he detects a colourful sailing boat gently bobbing up and down. I ask the client to observe this rhythmic rise and fall action and suggest that as he does this, the effect is one of intensifying his relaxation.

For clients who are not good at using their imagination, repeated suggestions that they will relax progressively more deeply, or deepening as the hypnotist counts down from ten with the greatest depth being achieved as the count is completed and the hypnotist says the word '*NOW*', can work quite effectively.

## Ego strengthening

The technique of 'ego strengthening' is a very useful one and is used in most programmes of hypnotherapy. It can be used as early as the first session but the clinical reality usually makes it possible only from the second session onwards. Hartland (op. cit.) states that a deep trance is not a prerequisite of this technique. However, he acknowledges that the deeper the trance the more rapid the improvement. Clients who respond to a pre-conditioned signal and readily enter a trance state are likely to achieve the necessary depth. It is basically a 'confidence boosting' or 'ego-assertive' (Waxman, 1981) technique, and is used to reassure the client that he will be able to handle previously difficult situations and that this will be facilitated by the therapeutic techniques employed during the sessions, whichever they might have been, whether under hypnosis or not. So, for example, if behaviour modification has been employed outside hypnosis, suggestions to the client that he will be able to use these techniques to deal with appropriate situations, can be made during an ego-strengthening routine. Before any routine is started, the therapist should discuss with and explain to the client the objectives, rationale and nature of the routine.

There is no magical formula for an ego-strengthening routine. It is really very much what one would say to any client or friend who needs encouragement and reassurance. Many hypnosis trainees soon become dependent on the handouts they are given with a suggested wording. If the principles of the technique are well understood, there is no reason why a therapist should not develop the 'patter' that comes most naturally to him and with which he feels most comfortable. There are however, several types of suggestions that are recommended. The suggestions made should convey that clients will be able to handle situations 'imaginally' in the first instance and during the trance state. Post-hypnotic suggestions can be made that the client will be able to deal with real situations with positive feelings.

Through ego strengthening, one can reassure the client that he will be able to confront problems in a confident manner and that there is no need to feel anxious. One should also encourage a client to look at such 'problems' in an objective fashion. Very often a client may perceive an issue as a problem because he has not objectively evaluated the matter. Perceiving the issue as problem-generating, he may then label it a problem and, in effect, that is what it becomes for him. When encouraged to rationalise his anxiety or fear, and when suggestions are made to him about how a problem may be resolved, a client may produce ingenious counteractive reasons to substantiate his perceptions. This behaviour may be quite revealing as it could be indicative of a client's resistance to wishing to resolve his problems, in any case at that moment of time. Its implications for therapy need to be considered carefully. For example, if the client is not ready to face his problems, one should not insist that he should, and the issue can be reintroduced at a later date. Assertive training can also form part of an ego-strengthening routine.

Hartland suggests that the hypnotherapist should pay particular attention to several factors when using an ego-strengthening routine. He believes that 'rhythm, repetition, interpolation of appropriate pauses and the stressing of certain important words and phrases are all essential.' These strategies are all aimed at giving more stress to the suggestions made. A suggestion can be repeated employing different wording to avoid monotony. Key words and phrases may be preceded by a pause and also intonationally stressed because of their significance to the client.

Clearly, there are some general guidelines about the substance of an ego-strengthening routine. The therapist, however, has to be very well prepared and have a good grasp of the client's needs and his problems in order to make such a technique effective. The routine thus, has to be tailor-made for the particular client and his problems. This is why, it may be too early to use the technique in the first session.

A typical routine may thus, start with some preparatory statements which would be more condusive to the client's receptivity of subsequent ones more related to the problem.

> "You have now become *so* deeply relaxed (pause) *so* deeply asleep (pause) that your mind has become *so* sensitive (pause) *so* receptive to what I say (pause) that *everything* that I put into your mind (pause) will sink *so* deeply into the unconscious part of your mind (pause) and will cause *so* deep and lasting an impression there .... that *nothing* will eradicate it." [The words in italics are stressed]     (Hartland, op. cit.)

Further preparatory instructions then assure the client that because he is so relaxed etc., the following suggestions will "begin to exercise a greater influence over the way you think ... over the way you feel ... over the way you behave."

Other phrases such as "the way you deal with your problem" can be added. The idea is to indicate to the client that he will experience a gradual change over the way he thinks, feels and acts.

Hartland's routine then enters a post-hypnotic suggestion stage when the client is told that the suggestions "will remain firmly embedded in the unconscious part of your mind...." and will be "*just* as strongly ... *just* as surely ... *just* as powerfully effective away from the clinical situation as they are during the session".

The routine is then followed with a reiteration that the suggestions "will" be experienced by the patient in "*exactly*" the way the hypnotherapist says and that they will do so "*just* as surely" etc., away from the clinical situation as during it. This reiteration not only serves to drive the message home but also allows the client time to process it (see Appendix for more details).

By this point, the client should be ready for the 'ego-strengthening' suggestions pertinent to the problem. Again, the hypnotherapist suggests that the client will be psychologically prepared to deal with the problem (though the use of 'emotive' and 'negative' terms such as 'psychologically' and 'problem' are not advised) and to look at it objectively. This will help the client to handle any situation with more confidence and in a more relaxed and assertive manner. The suggestions during this phase become more positive and definitive and more problem-centred. The routine may end with a description to the client of the benefits of the suggestions "... you will feel *much happier* (pause) much *more contented, much more optimistic* in every way as the treatment programme progresses, and consequently you will become less dependent on other people for the resolution of your problem."

## Post-hypnotic suggestion

Post-hypnotic suggestion is probably the most valuable aid in hypnotherapy and usually works best for clients who have achieved a medium to deep trance. It can be an effective technique in "conditioning" clients to respond to a stimulus, verbal or otherwise, and enter a trance state without the need to go through the whole trance induction routine. Under hypnosis, it is suggested to the client that on the next encounter he will be able to enter the same trance depth as he is experiencing now, in response to a verbal instruction "(Client's name) .... let go."

Other stimuli could be in the form of touching the client's forehead, or back of neck, or a firm nod from the hypnotist, etc. The client is reassured that he will not respond to any of these stimuli if given by anyone else and even if the hypnotist himself produces any of these stimuli in any other situation other than when the client comes for hypnosis. It is important that this reassurance is given just in case the client and hypnotist meet in a different situation and inadvertently the hypnotist, for example, nods his head. This is why, I prefer to use a stimulus which I am not likely to use unwittingly at 'non-appropriate' times.

Post-hypnotic suggestions are also used in hypnotherapy, for example, during ego-strengthening routines (see above), to help a client respond positively whilst in the wake state to situations known to contribute or exacerbate his problem. The client can therefore, be encouraged to achieve a certain independence from the hypnotist and control over his behaviour. The client, in the wake state, might well be aware that a post-hypnotic suggestion has been made and may even recall its nature in great detail but when faced with the appropriate stimulus find it difficult not to comply with it. Resistance to post-hypnotic suggestion is possible but often requires great effort on behalf of the client. Unlike what was previously believed, amnesia is not a prerequisite for effective post-hypnotic suggestion though it can increase its strength. When rejection of a post-hypnotic suggestion takes place, it is likely to be because the client finds it ridiculous, unreasonable or illogical. In addition, sometimes a client may find a post-hypnotic suggestion, threatening and this may manifest in the client's verbal and/or physical behaviour indicating discomfort or distress. It is therefore, important for the hypnotist to monitor the client's reactions whilst the suggestions are being given. If appropriate, such suggestions can be rewarded or even aborted.

Sometimes the client's full attention needs to be obtained before a post-hypnotic suggestion is realized. On occasions, he may have an intense distraction such as wishing to speak about something which he has been burning to say, and may consequently not correctly interpret or perceive the stimulus. Post-hypnotic suggestions should therefore, be as precisely worded as possible. The hypnotist must also make the suggestions with confidence and conviction. Repeating post-hypnotic suggestions during any one routine and also over a period of sessions is more likely to make them durable. Post-hypnotic suggestions no longer appropriate should be removed.

The problem with post-hypnotic suggestion is that its effect often diminishes with time. The hypnotist should capitalise on the time during which post-hypnotic suggestions are effective to enhance its effects, perhaps by employing other therapeutic techniques. Waxman (op. cit.) however, reports a client responding to a post-hypnotic suggestion given 15 years earlier.

## Auto-hypnosis

Encouraging a client to be self-reliant is very important and this should be done as early as possible during therapy. Whereas techniques such as post-hypnotic suggestion and ego stregthening can be very effective in helping a client to deal with problems when away from the hypnotist's care, an additional strategy for the client is his ability to hypnotise himself at appropriate times. Clients invariably need explanation of the nature and uses of auto-hypnosis and training in developing the skill. Some clients may never be able to achieve this skill. The first question they are likely to ask is whether there is a danger in not being able to wake themselves up. Clients should be assured that they will be able to do this in the same way as they were responsible for putting themselves in a trance. The worst that can happen is that they get so relaxed that they fall asleep and in time, wake up in the usual way. They can be told that auto-hypnosis is in fact an experience that most people have had, for example, when nodding off in front of the television or just simply relaxing.

Training in auto-hypnosis is best done whilst the client is in hypnosis under the care of the hypnotist. Using post-hypnotic suggestion, the hypnotist tells the client that whenever he feels it is necessary he will be able to put himself in a trance. When the need arises, he can either lie down or sit himself on a comfortable chair and close his eyes. He will then imagine himself in the hypnotist's rooms and recall the induction routine just as if the hypnotist were sitting by his side.

Advising the client that he can screw his eyes up or clench his fist tightly, and then relaxing them after counting down from five, could be a useful trigger. This in fact could be used by the hypnotist during the induction routine. As the eyes or fist relax, so the relaxation will then radiate from that point throughout the client's body until he is totally relaxed. When he wishes to wake up, all he has to do is to count down from five again and as he counts, suggest to himself that he is slowly waking up and will open his eyes when he finishes counting. The client should be told that he will only attempt auto-hypnosis when it is safe and not when he needs to be very alert such as when driving. He should also be told, that when in auto-hypnosis, he will always remain alert to any occurrence needing his attention so that if the doorbell or telephone rings, for example, he will, if he feels necessary, be able to wake up and attend to it. The client is encouraged to practise self-hypnosis in the hypnotist's presence and then at the beginning and end of the day but always at a time which will be free from distraction.

*Case Study 1*

The power of auto-hypnosis is illustrated by this case. Ruth, a female client attended for hypnosis to lose weight. She was an excellent subject and learned auto-hypnosis quite quickly. The effectiveness was tested one day when on returning from a car trip in France, she refused to get onto the Cross Channel Ferry because "a very strong wind" was blowing. Her husband desperately suggested she should try self-hypnosis which she agreed to do. She went on board, sat herself down on a seat on deck and just before the ferry's departure went into self-hypnosis. She reported that even though she could hear the waiters dropping trays etc., she managed the crossing without any anxiety or fear at all and to everyone's surprise, and one might add, relief.

Auto-hypnosis can also be taught without the use of post-hypnotic suggestion and through an eye-fixation technique. The hypnotist asks the client to imagine himself at home or any other suitable place. The hypnotist should then induce the client into a hypnotic trance and encourage him to relax. Once this is achieved the client is brought out of hypnosis and without any discussion of the experience, is told to imagine himself in the type of environment that he is likely to be in when in future he practises auto-hypnosis. Once in this situation, and sitting on a chair of his choice, or lying down, he is to commence the self-hypnosis routine. The easiest method for most clients is usually eye-fixation with progressive relaxation. The client is thus told to fix his gaze on a point above his head or straight ahead. He is then instructed to repeat silently to himself all the suggestions that the hypnotist is making whilst he is again taken through the induction routine but to do so in the first person. For example:

HYPNOTIST: "As I gaze at the point I have chosen, I will soon feel my eyes getting heavier and heavier."

CLIENT: "As I gaze at the point I have chosen, I will soon feel my eyes" etc.

After eye closure, the client continues 'shadowing' the hypnotist's suggestions of progressive relaxation, always in the first person. Once relaxation is achieved, the client can bring himself out of hypnosis with positive suggestions of well being, and so on. This routine has to be practised again but this time the client does so on his own, indicating with a finger response when he reaches each stage. The hypnotist can then help him on to the next stage.

Auto-hypnosis can also be taught by explaining the routine to the client whilst he is still awake. The hypnotist goes through all the suggestions that the client has to give himself from beginning to end, including those he needs to give himself to achieve relaxation, ego strengthening, and eventually, termination to the wake state. Some clients may need to have all these directions repeated before they attempt to put themselves in hypnosis. Daily practice is absolutely essential before they become proficient in the self-hypnosis skill. Some clients may not achieve the task the first few times but practice usually leads to success. It is essential at the beginning of each subsequent session to discuss with the client how he fared with his attempts at auto-hypnosis so that the hypnotist can montor his progress and can give advice as appropriate. It is also essential for the client to demonstrate to the hypnotist how he has been practising by actually going into auto-hypnosis during each session and in the hypnotist's presence.

Very few clients achieve more than a medium trance in auto-hypnosis, probably because they need to retain a certain amount of conscious control and activity in order to give themselves the necessary instructions and monitor their outcome. However, some clients are able to employ deepening techniques such as arm rigidity, through auto-suggestion. Similarly, they may also be able to use the type of hypnotherapeutic strategies that the hypnotist has employed with them, for conditions such as pain control, respiratory control in asthma, confidence boosting, stress and anxiety reduction, etc..

*Case Study 2*

James, a paraplegic health professional who suffered intermittent but excrutiating 'phantom' pains in his legs, acquired auto-hypnosis skills to control these pains, whilst he attended one of our three day hypnotherapy workshops. When we were practising inducing analgesia, he enquired whether it was possible to get rid of pain which did not have a physiological basis, such as his 'phantom' pain. Having obtained his agreement, he was put into a medium trance, and the routine to induce analgesia on his legs which he said were aching at the time, was started. Suggestions were thus given to him that as his legs were being gently rubbed, so his pain would be squeezed out, much like toothpaste is squeezed out of a tube, and disappear into the air. On awakening, he could not believe that his pain had indeed gone. Next day, he reported that the pain had returned in the evening and that he was able to get rid of it through auto-hypnotically induced analgesia.

When hypnotherapy or auto-hypnosis is used for pain control, one must ensure that it is only employed for pains which do not require medical supervision. Pain is often the body's way of indicating some physical or physiological malfunction. If the client can achieve self-induced analgesia, he may in fact be removing the one alarm which may signal a serious organic problem. The cause of the pain should therefore, be medically diagnosed and understood and the hypnotist must impose restrictions on the particular type of pain which can be relieved safely through auto-hypnosis. The hypnotist must also advise the client not to attempt any self hypno-analytical techniques without any competent supervision.

## Hypno-analytic techniques

Hypno-analytic techniques are used in order to establish the genesis of a problem and its subsequent development. In the hands of a properly qualified hypnotherapist, these techniques can be very useful and suggest the form of subsequent therapy. Clients who have experienced such analytic techniques may enhance their awareness of the cause and nature of their problem and this in itself may have profound therapeutic effects. It can not be stressed strongly enough, however, that the therapists with little experience of psychopathology and psychotherapy should not attempt to use hypno-analytic techniques. The revelation of deeply suppressed memories can be very traumatic to clients, and helping clients to resolve these requires expert management. There is perhaps one justification in including this topic in this chapter rather than in Chapter 4 and this is that on occasions, clients may recall a traumatic memory under a hypnotic trance on their own accord. It is important that a hypnotist recognises when this is happening and understands the dynamics of the experience. For those hypnotherapists who have the relevant psychological qualifications or experience, a knowledge of hypno-analytic techniques is essential.

### *Regression Analysis*

The principle behind regression analysis is predominantly based on psychoanalytic theory though there is no doubt that its rationale can also be explained by other schools of psychological thought. The basic assumption is that a client's problems may have their origin in an earlier experience. Whether this early experience has subsequently resulted in a form of behaviour manifested by the problem (behaviourist theory) or whether the problem has been caused by unresolved and suppressed conflicts/ experiences (psychoanalytic theory) is perhaps not of crucial importance. In regression analysis, clients are encouraged to either recall or re-enact relevant early causal experiences. Usually, a deep trance is necessary for age regression.

Before regression analysis is attempted, its nature and objectives should be explained to clients and their agreement and co-operation secured. It is important that the hypnotherapist knows the client's exact age and date of birth. Once this is established, a trance is induced, if necessary deepened, and then the IMR is established. The client is told that a two-way verbal conversation with the hypnotherapist is possible. The process is then introduced with words such as

> "NOW (client's name) you remember we discussed the question of trying, whilst you were under hypnosis, to see if you can recall an early experience which may be related to your problem. To do so, we need to take you back to an earlier stage in your life. In a few moments now, we shall attempt to do this. If at any point you do not wish to proceed with this exercise you can say so verbally."

It is often useful to establish an IMR in both hands, one to signal affirmative responses and the other negative ones. If this has been done, the client can be told

> ".... you can also signal your wish not to proceed by indicating it by ..... (whatever IMR has been established)"

Several approaches can now be taken. A client can be asked to "free float" into an age which may be associated with the problem, or helped to age regress year by year. The process can be shortened somewhat for older clients by asking them to regress in batches of five years.

If a free-floating strategy is employed, the client is told that once the relevant age is reached, this will be indicated by the IMR. At this point, the client is asked to tell the hypnotherapist what age is being recalled. Further description of the relevant memory/experience is then requested by the hypnotherapist. In order to help clients regress, the trigger word PAST can be used, signifying the passage of time.

If the second or third strategy is chosen, clients can be helped to regress by the hypnotherapist saying

> "You are now at the present time and you are (client's actual age). We are now going to help you go back in time and to do so I shall mention the different ages ... "

At this point, it may be useful to employ a strategy called a 'diagnostic scan'. The objective of this is to allow clients to go back in time and from then forwards to their actual age without feeling that they have to reveal or confront any memory/experience. The hypnotherapist should then continue something like this:

> ".... As we go back in time you may come to an age when you have had an experience which could be related to the present problem. If this happens, your sub-conscious mind will indicate it by the IMR/raising the index finger of your right hand ...."

The hypnotherapist then signals the passing of time by saying "... you are now going to go back to when you were ...." - the age will depend on how many years at a time the client is to be regressed. After a few moments to allow the client to regress to that age, the hypnotherapist says " .... you are now X years of age .... X years of age .... you are now X years." The hypnotherapist should monitor the client's facial expression or any other bodily movement which may indicate the client's feelings as regression continues. Clients may first show signs of distress in this way rather than through a verbal response. If the client shows distress, the hypnotherapist can either continue the regression or ask the client if it will help to talk about any experiences that occurred at that age.

Whatever the client says must be respected. Because verbal responses are sometimes sluggish, the client must be given ample time to respond. If it is clear that the client does not wish to talk, the hypnotherapist can say

".... it seems that you can not or do not wish to tell me about your experiences at that age .... we may come back to them another time when you are ready. In the meantime, let us continue going back in time."

As the diagnostic scan proceeds, the hypnotherapist should make a written note of the ages indicated by the IMR. The regression should be stopped at a suitable age, often indicated by the case history data. For example, a client can be asked during interview to estimate or guess an approximate age at which the problem may have started. When this point is reached, the client is advanced in age in the same way as he was regressed and using the same intervals. Again the hypnotherapist notes down the ages signalled by the IMR. This provides a double check. When the actual age is reached the client should be reassured and if showing any tension or distress, relaxed. The client should be congratulated for co-operating and told that soon he will be woken up and will feel relaxed and safe. The trance state is then terminated.

Once the client is awake, discussion can take place as to the significance of those ages. Sometimes clients' memories have been brought back and they are able to discuss them quite lucidly and sometimes with a sense of humour. It is not unusual for clients to express relief at linking a past experience with their present problem. This in itself can be very therapeutic. Other clients may in fact be aware that they went back to a significant age when they suffered some trauma, but find it difficult to pinpoint what this was. Such clients are usually suppressing distressing memories and may not be ready to confront them.

The diagnostic scan is thus, useful to locate likely problem-related ages but may not necessarily reveal any detail. It may take several sessions before a client may be prepared to be regressed to those ages and try to recall or re-enact any relevant experiences. Dealing with such experiences requires skill and training and a hypnotherapist is often not able to predict the intensity of the client's reaction. However, some clients may experience immediate benefit.

*Case Study 3*

Dora was 50 years old, 5 foot 2 inches tall and weighed 14 and a half stones. Her weight was causing her a lot of distress. She was unable to go on diets prescribed by her GP and only felt secure if her pockets were full of sweets and chocolates which she would 'gobble' down at every opportunity. Her personal life was also very stressful as she had to care for a husband suffering with multiple sclerosis. Her doctor on her request, referred her for hypnosis confirming that in his view there were no psychiatric or medical reasons to contra-indicate this course.

Dora was a cheerful lady and co-operated fully with the first induction technique tried. She agreed to go on the 'Scarsdale Medical Diet' for two weeks. At the second session she reported she had been doing well. However, her husband had had a 'bad turn' on the sixth day, a Sunday, and she found herself picking at the Sunday meals she was preparing for the family. Consequently, she had only achieved a nett loss of half a pound.

When asked, she said she could not help it and she knew she was not keeping her agreement. She could not think of any childhood experience which might explain this behaviour. It seemed however, that this was a typical pattern for her, and anytime she was under stress she would 'gorge' herself.

She agreed to regression analysis and successfully regressed to age eight. At this point she recalled the experience of returning home from school on her own. Her mother was 'a career woman' and both she and Dora's father were at work until six in the afternoon. She recalled how she let herself in with a key hidden under a brick. Her home was Victorian - cold, big and with high ceilings. She was always very scared to be at home on her own. Even though she was never hungry at that time of the day, she invariably made a beeline for the kitchen and 'stuffed herself with food'.

Brought back to her actual age and out of her trance, she smiled and showed amazement at having recalled an experience she had completely forgotten about. She immediately made the link between this experience and her over-eating, especially during stressful situations. She had never told her mother about her feelings and felt a little guilty that she still seemed to carry that grudge albeit subconsciously about her having been 'a career woman'. She agreed that it would help her if she could now tell her now 74 year old mother how she had felt in her childhood. She subsequently did so and was surprised that her mother did not get annoyed at being told and had been unaware of her dislike at being left on her own at home for part of the afternoon. The "confession" helped Dora to get rid of her guilty feelings about her mother.

This experience must have helped her and she was then able to continue her diet without panicking every time her husband had a relapse. By the end of the second week she had lost 3 1/2 pounds and another three by the end of the third week. She felt she was now in control of her diet and could continue on her own. She agreed to keep in telephone contact and reported having lost a stone and a half on her last phone contact and six and a half weeks since first seen.

## Structured Dream Analysis

This technique is useful when a client may find it difficult or may not be ready to recall early experiences. Many clients may find after an induction session that they become more aware that they dream at night. In structured dream analysis, the client is told that dreams will become clearer and that they will be recalled much better for discussion at the next session. If this happens, the hypnotherapist can, at the next encounter suggest to the client under hypnosis what the nature of dreams for the next week will be. These, it is suggested, will be more related to the client's present problems. The following week, the nature and significance of the dreams can be discussed. This technique may then suggest a management strategy for the client's problem.

A variation of this technique involves suggesting to the client that he will have a dream whilst in a trance, and just before awakening. The client can be directed as to the subject of the dream and encouraged to relate it and if possible interpret it, whilst it is being experienced. Interpreting such dreams whilst in a trance is much more effective than when awake.

## Hypnopictography

Another technique found useful to help overcome repression involves inducing a deep trance in the client. At some appropriate point, the client is told that in a few moments a sketch pad or other suitable writing material will be placed on his lap and he will be given a pencil. The client will then be told that on opening his eyes, he will draw anything that comes to mind. If considered appropriate the subject of the drawing can be suggested by the hypnotherapist and this can be related to whatever experience the client is recalling while regressed at a certain age. The client can be told that the drawing will reflect a story related to that experience.

An interesting characteristic of hypnopictography is that most clients will not raise the pen from the paper as the drawing develops and will sometimes even continue drawing beyond the page boundary. If the latter happens, he can be helped to return to the page surface. The client can either be asked to explain and interpret the drawing as it progresses or can be asked to do so in the wake state.

## Other Analytic Techniques

There are several other analytic techniques such as play therapy, Wolberg's 'Theatre Visualisation', and Redlich's 'Jigsaw Puzzle Visualisation' techniques. Further details of these techniques can be found in Hartland (op. cit.), Rowley (1986) and Waxman (op. cit.).

None of these techniques should be practised by the 'amateur' psychotherapist. Most clients are only likely to 'recall' memories. A very small number usually 'relive' their memories in which case they will behave exactly as they used to when they were actually the age they are regressed to. Some clients may 'abreact' when they recall and re-enact, not only long repressed and painful memories, but also the emotional effects associated with the events recalled. The results are often very distressing. Even though Hartland (op. cit.) states that "true abreaction is a rare occurrence," a hypnotherapist using hypno-analytic techniques must be qualified to deal with the consequences, both during the client's behaviour in the trance state, and later on during the waking state.

Hypno-analytic experiences can also be used in hypnotherapy. One other warning must be unequivocally given. These techniques can be very powerful and though rarely, can sometimes have tragic results. A case was reported of a depressive client who was told that he no longer needed to be depressed. On waking, he felt so euphoric to the point of becoming manic. He also developed delusions that he could fly and attempted to prove this by taking off from a third floor window and killing himself. Whether this would have happened sooner or later, and whether this tragedy was a direct result of hypnosis, was not conclusively explained.

## Termination

Ending a hypnotic trance in an appropriate way is very important. I have witnessed several hypnotherapists not doing so with the consequence that a client may come out of hypnosis in a certain state of disorientation or confusion. It is a fact that many subjects experience certain perceptual distortions during hypnosis, particularly time 'disorientation'.

If regression has been used, the therapist must ensure that the client is 'brought up' to his current age. Failure to do this may, on occasions, leave the wake subject behaving at the regressed age. If this were to happen, the client should be induced back to hypnosis, and then brought back to his actual age. Any ideomotor responses established under hypnosis, must be 'cancelled' by saying to the client during the termination phase, that he will no longer respond, by raising his index finger, for example, to the stimulus previously used, nor when he wishes to indicate whichever response had previously been associated with the IMR. If this is not done, a client may find later on in the day perhaps, that in conversation he is surprised to witness his finger going up when, say, responding in the affirmative to someone's question.

It is also important to tell the client that he will only respond to trance inducing techniques or post-hypnotic suggestions "when in an appropriate situation with the hypnotherapist." It is essential to keep the basis of this instruction intact because some clients may feel anxious that if they meet the hypnotherapist in any other situation, the latter will be able to exercise undue influence during a non-clinical encounter. This is especially true when there is a possibility that clients will be encountered outside the clinical situation, for example socially, or, in small communities, in several other situations.

In order to counteract the effect of any perceptual distortions of time, place etc., one should tell the client that when he wakes up he will find himself in the room or location he started off in, in the company of the therapist and anyone else who was there at the start of the session, or who came in during the session. It is also good practice to remind the client of the full date (including the year) and the time of the day. On occasions, it may be appropriate not to inform him of the time but ask him when awake if he knows how long he has been in the trance state and then tell him the exact time. This might be useful when for good reason, the therapist may wish to find out if any time distortion has taken place or when subjects have previously shown incredulity of the amount of time the trance state has lasted. This is especially useful for clients who have declared that they are not able to 'relax' for more than a very short time.

Most clients feel very relaxed when they are brought out of a trance, almost lethargic. I have therefore, always made it my practice, especially if they are driving, to instruct them that when they open their eyes and come out of their trance they will feel relaxed and refreshed but that they will remain alert to anything which requires their attention; that they will drive with due care and attention, and so on. The client is then brought out of the trance with instructions such as

> "In a few moments time I shall be counting down from 5. When I finish counting, I will say the word *NOW* (or any other trigger word) and you will open your eyes and come out of this trance. When you do so, you will find yourself in my [room and if necessary, address]. You will see me [and anyone else in the room] and we shall be talking about your experience. So, very soon now, I shall be counting down from 5. When you open your eyes, you will feel relaxed and refreshed but you will always be alert to anything requiring your attention ["you will drive with due care and attention"]. Today is [full date] and it is now [time]. I am going to start counting now and when I finish counting, I will say the word *NOW* and you will open your eyes and come out of hypnosis. So —— 5, 4, 3, 2, 1, *NOW!*"

Following termination, a client may need a little while to become fully attentive; this usually takes a matter of a few minutes. Once fully awake, a post session discussion should take place to allow the client to provide feedback about his experience to the therapist, or ask any questions. The therapist in turn may be interested in the client's view about how useful and effective the particular induction and deepening technique used was, how the client feels it may be modified to provide greater benefit, were there any experiences or sensations the client did not like, how deep did the client feel had the trance been, and so on. It is sometimes useful, following this discussion, to set goals for the next session so that the client does not need to be kept in what could be anxiety-producing suspense.

# CHAPTER 4
# Hypnotherapy in the Management of Psychologically Related Problems

## Malcolm J. W. Hughes & Samuel Abudarham

'Psychologically-related' problems include those frequently referred to as psychosomatic conditions though not all psychologically-related problems are necessarily psychosomatic. For many decades, it has long been appreciated that the individual's moods can reflect the working, both normal or abnormal, of the body, and conversely, that mood can adversely affect the harmonious functioning of the body.

The term 'psychosomatic' has been applied in several different ways. When referring to 'psychosomatic disorders', it is usually implied that there exist certain specific illnesses which reflect a definite organic pathology and whose origins are psychologically determined. In these instances, emotional stress, both short and long term by nature, are thought to play a major role. The conditions associated with stressful origins include certain cases of asthma, some forms of dermatitis and eczema, migraine, essential hypertension, ulcerative colitis and peptic and duodenal ulcers.

It is possible to expand this list by including such conditions as coronary artery disease, paroxysmal tachycardia, anorexia nervosa, bulimia and others. Recent evidence goes further to suggest that conditions considered to be clearly organic by nature e.g. cancer, are now considered in certain instances to have a 'psychosomatic' link. Hence, it is sometimes more appropriate to talk of a 'psychosomatic' approach to illness conditions, thereby implying, perhaps more realistically, that many illness conditions have a psychological dimension, this having the effect of contributing to the onset and progress of the condition as well as determining the individual's effective rate of recovery from the condition.

In terms of the precipitating factors in psychosomatic conditions, the identification of psychological and social variables contributing to the causation of human morbidity has been of prime concern. Current research is based on the experience of individuals' life events, based upon their social environment, together with their intrapsychic and overt behavioural responses to such events. Under given circumstances, based upon variables including environmental factors, personality, emotional experiences, stressful episodes and, in some cases, experience of previous illness conditions, a person may be found to be predisposed to a variety of diseases, ranging from mild to severe in their effect.

One of the major questions asked with respect to such psychosomatic illnesses is by what manner may stressful and emotional experiences, registered at a 'psychological' level, become modified and subsequently identified as a 'physical' condition? Considerable research has been conducted over recent years in an attempt to answer this question, and two possible factors are indicated as likely pathways (Brown and Heninger, 1976; Latimer, 1979; Schleifer et al, 1983).

In the first instance, a recognised link between neurological function and endocrine (hormonal) responses has become evident. Much of the human endocrine function is controlled from the pituitary gland, a structure suspended from below the central, mid-brain region (the hypothalamus). Part of the pituitary is rich in nerve fibres from the brain and will therefore, be susceptible to variations in neurone stimulation, due in turn to variations in brain activity. Such changes are likely to cause an alteration in the synthesis and secretion of hormones, or hormone stimulating agents in the pituitary which in turn, affect the physiological functioning of the body. Research (Theorell, 1970; Cobb et al, 1974; Khansari et al, 1990) has indicated that it is primarily the steroid hormones, in particular those released from the adrenal cortex, that under conditions of prolonged stress will precipitate physiological changes resulting in a variety of illness conditions.

In these circumstances, the adverse effect is due not only to an increased or prolonged secretion of such hormones, but also to a failure of the body system to metabolise and thereby inactivate the hormones once they have exerted their physiological effect. Consequently, the physiological imbalance which results can and does exert a strain on any number of other body systems, leading to various morbidity states.

The second system likely to result in a conversion factor from human emotional states to physical ailments, is what is referred to as the 'psycho-immunological' response. Studies in this area of medical research are not as clearly defined as with endocrine responses. Nevertheless, there exists evidence to suggest that psycho-social stress can in turn, cause a change in the body's immune functioning ( Stein at al, 1976; Hughes, 1984, 1985; Martin, 1987; Khansari et al, op. cit.) The general effect results in components of the immune system, known as immunoglobulins (Ig) altering with respect to each other. When this happens, some of the immunoglobulins remain unchanged whilst others may increase or decrease in concentration, depending on factors such as the condition itself and the individual's response to it and any resultant stress. For example, studies of medical students and non-psychotic psychiatric inpatients have indicated that loneliness may result in the suppression of natural killer (NK) cell activity. Solomon (1981) found a number of immunological abnormalities in schizophrenics.

Any resulting immunoglobin imbalance tends to have a detrimental effect on the system, leading to a weakening of the person's natural defences to infection. Consequently, the milder effects of this can be the onset of a viral infection, such as the common cold.

Allowing for the likely effects of both psycho-endocrine and psycho-immune responses on an individual, it has been pointed out that many illnesses regarded as psychosomatic are also those which have a strong hereditary element. There exists therefore, a possibility that patients who develop these conditions may have some latent constitutional defect which breaks down under conditions of stress, and results in illness. This is a point mentioned by Adler (1966) in his theory of 'organ inferiority'. Similar concepts are expressed in other areas of research based largely on embryological and neonatal studies (Broussard, 1976; Eisenberg, 1977; Stratton, 1977).

Adler (op. cit.) implied that if some part of the body was markedly 'weaker' than the rest, then when stressed, the entire body system would strive to compensate for this deficiency. In the case of a psychogenic stress-induced illness, this process could go too far, resulting in the individual overcompensating for his disability. This in turn can result in his drives being neurotically determined, leading to secondary stresses which can generate excessive pressures on the weak organ, or on the mind, with consequent psychosomatic or even psychiatric illness.

If we are to accept the above hypothesis and consider that the mechanisms underlying these types of disorders are essentially similar, one might expect an excessive tendency for both kinds of illnesses to occur in the same people. In some instances, this is the case; some individuals do suffer both mental and physical disorders following stressful episodes in their lives. An interesting explanation for this is what has been referred to as "illness clustering" (Hinkle, 1961). A "clustering" effect was observed in which an obvious pattern was established between the patient's exposure to stressful episodes which were followed, within approximately a three month period, by symptom onset and various physical illnesses.

Many people appear to go through phases in their lives when they are unduly likely to develop illnesses, either physical or mental. When such phases occur, it is often impossible to decide whether one illness leads to another or whether there exists some underlying factor which predisposes the persons thus affected to any kind of disease. In a study of 300 patients in general practice, matched with controls who had not had cause to be referred to their doctors (Hughes, 1979), a "clustering" effect was observed. Further investigation showed patients exposed to stressful and emotive life events during a given period, developed symptoms and in turn, registered an increase in consultations within the subsequent three months. Further analysis suggested that consultations by these patients within a period of two to three months, were predictive of further consultations with the doctor later. This suggests that the patients' decision to self-refer was due to either a concern over the symptom, or to a consequence of the stressful episodes, or both. In the majority of cases, it was found that the illness clusters observed in this instance were determined largely by short term stressful life episodes together with the associated anxiety related to such episodes.

## Psychosomatic repertoire

A further feature which has been noted in some individuals is the 'psychosomatic repertoire', in which the patient is noted to have a series of psychosomatic-type disorders either simultaneously or consecutively. These may sometimes be interspersed with other physical or psychiatric conditions, in the latter case, depression being an obvious feature. Such a response may be indicative of some fundamental nervous instability or, in some cases, simply be a multiple response to a number of causative factors.

When confronted with this complex array of information, one might be justified in querying what best to do in treating such ailments. The obvious tendency might be to deal with the symptoms which manifest in such illness conditions. Whilst it is recognised that laboratory investigations and scientific methods of treatment, including prescribed medications, are as ever important, there has perhaps been an unfortunate tendency to overlook the patients themselves, in particular the influence that their fears and anxieties may have on the cause and development of their illness.

Apart from the humanitarian aspect of this approach, it could be claimed to represent sound medical practice. One is frequently faced with the patient presenting with a somatic disorder who undergoes treatment and, despite resolving the symptoms of that disorder, fails in a psychological sense to regain a sense of well-being. Not too infrequently, there exists an underlying, emotional problem or even a psychiatric condition which may be complicating if not prolonging the illness. In all likelihood, that very condition or problem may have precipitated the illness in the first place. Should this not be recognised, then the patient may well go on feeling unwell, either on a continuous or intermittent basis, be made to undergo unnecessary tests and investigations which in themselves can be stress inducing, and possibly result in a further deterioration of the person's health.

Hence, the inevitable question, what constitutes an appropriate form of treatment in the case of psychosomatic conditions? The very nature and variety of conditions which come under the title 'psychosomatic disorder' compounds the problem of treatment. Nevertheless, there does exist in many of these conditions a commmon underlying theme - the individual experiencing such conditions is likely at some time to have been exposed to a stressful life event, or events, which may in turn have caused anxiety, worry, frustration and an overall emotional strain. There is also strong evidence to suggest that, at the time of these episodes, the affected individuals would have been psychologically unprepared to confront the problems related to such events and thereby have failed to cope effectively for themselves.

## Hypnosis as a therapeutic approach

The concept of applying hypnosis as part of a supportive therapeutic approach has much to offer. Compared to other techniques or practices, e.g. psychoanalysis, insight therapy or direct treatment of the physical symptoms, this form of supportive therapy involves the likelihood of a stronger therapist-patient relationship. In addition, such support will include the means of providing the patient with the reassurance and encouragement, which when given under hypnosis, should not be underestimated (Hartland, 1971). The effectiveness of hypnosis in the treatment of certain organic illnesses has been recognised, but it has been shown to be even more effective when the illness has been shown to be accompanied by a strong emotional component, particularly in conditions such as asthma (Moore, 1965; Maher-Loughnan, 1970), hypertension (Deabler, 1973) and migraine (Basker et al, 1975).

In these instances, the effect on the patient is to modify his reactions to such symptoms, by lowering emotional and physical tension and by reducing any anxiety or fears resulting from any stressful episodes which may have contributed to the overall condition. Under such forms of therapy, it becomes necessary to encourage in the patient a strong faith in their ability to cope with, and in turn, overcome those stressors with which they identify. It is also essential to enable the patients to readjust themselves emotionally to everyday reality and their environment. To enforce this approach, whether hypnosis is a major element in the treatment or not, the therapist must come over as being outgoing and more verbally and affectively expressive.

When dealing with psychosomatic symptoms, it is recognised that factors such as tension, anxiety and apprehension constitute a direct influence on the nature and intensity of those symptoms, especially in the case of an individual's pain threshold. Pain control through the use of hypnosis may constitute part of the therapy regime employed (See also Chapter 6). In some instances, this means of reducing the effects of pain will in itself be an encouragement to the patient in the early stages of treatment. To this end, the therapist must establish a 'therapeutic alliance' with the patient; such an alliance should encompass the following:-

1. Establishing a state of rapport.
2. A positive transference, fostered by the therapist who is readily available when needed.
3. A state of mutual communication and understanding, where the therapist can set limits without being judgemental or showing punitive or intolerant attitudes.

Hartland recognises three main approaches in the therapeutic use of hypnosis, particularly for psychosomatic conditions. These take the form of:-

1. Hypnosis in symptom removal.
2. Hypnosis in simple psychotherapy.
3. Hypnosis in analytical psychotherapy.

In employing any of the above approaches, it is essential that prior to administering therapy, case-notes concerning the patient's past history, including previous medical history, must be compiled. Taking details of a patient's case history need not be an arduous task, particularly if the right questions have been thought out and are asked systematically. In certain instances, communication with the patient's own doctor may be necessary (See also Chapter 2).

## The clinical approach

### *Hypnosis in Relaxation*

The use of hypnosis with psychosomatic conditions relies heavily on the element of relaxation, in which there is a melting away of tensions and a minimisation of environmental and internal stimuli that could interfere with the experience. The importance of having the patient in as relaxed a state is twofold:

i)  A number of psychosomatic conditions are brought on through the experience of stressful episodes, reflecting on the part of the patient a perception of such episodes as to possibly increase their levels of anxiety and anticipatory responses which, in themselves, generate tension. Consequently, if such 'stressors' become frequent or prolonged, the likelihood of tension becoming more established is increased. Such a situation is exacerbated when there is a failure on the part of a patient to effectively cope with the stress-inducing circumstances.

ii)  In the main, hypnosis may be viewed as a state of relaxation, certainly in the initial stages of induction and deepening. Thus, the therapist would be inducing a relaxed state in the patient as part of the hypnotic process. To be fully effective and beneficial to the patient, the relaxation must be sufficiently established to both induce the hypnotic state as well as alleviate the tension that has established itself in the patient. Hence, both basic inductive techniques, incorporating progressive relaxation, together with deepening tend to be employed at each session. The general tendency is for the patient to relax more effectively the more they experience this approach on each successive consultation.

Where efforts have been made to induce relaxation and feelings of bodily comfort, considerable improvements in physiological function become apparent. Relaxation, accompanied by visual imagery and suggesting a sense of heaviness and warmth initiates a series of changes including regular and comfortable cardiac and respiratory effects, and warmth in the abdominal region.

Such effects become especially pertinent when used among a particular clientele. As an example, trials involving asthmatic patients (Maher-Loughnan et al, 1962) demonstrated significant improvements when given hypnotherapy at lengthening intervals but at the same time employing self-hypnosis, i.e. relaxation techniques, on a daily basis. Similar beneficial results were obtained in a controlled investigation of hypertension (Deabler op. cit., 1973). Treatment was solely by hypnosis, and significant lowering of both systolic and diastolic blood pressure was observed.

The techniques involved at this stage of treatment tend to include the following four basic elements:

1) A mental approach, such as gazing fixedly at an object or silently or audibly repeating a phrase, word or sound; the result of these procedures is to shift from logical external-orientated thought.
2) The adoption of a passive attitude in which distracting thought should be disregarded - emphasising to the patient that "thoughts will drift in and out of your mind, but they are of no importance at this moment".
3) The decrease of muscle tone – the patient adopts a comfortable posture so that no muscular effort is required.
4) A quiet environment with decreased environmental stimuli.

When the techniques employed in producing such relaxation responses are used, the physiological parameters alter in a comparable fashion. In general, oxygen consumption, heart rate and respiratory rate all show a decrease. In white clients, there may also be a noticeable change in the pallor of the skin, in some instances.

In considering the effects of induced relaxation on a group of psychosomatic patients, Frankel and Misch (1973) commented on some patients reporting gastro-intestinal symptoms, including difficulty with control of bowel movements. The conditions identified included ulcerative colitis (e.g. Crohn's disease) and diarrhoea. Their hypnotherapy focussed largely on relaxation and the relaxation technique was made part of a self-induced experience. The patients were instructed to roll their eyes up, slowly close their eyelids, breathe in deeply and exhale after holding their breath for a few seconds. On exhaling, they were instructed to let all the muscles of their head, neck, shoulders, arms, body and lower limbs relax. Once a state of relaxation was achieved, they were then instructed to imagine themselves floating or gliding, and to concentrate their attention to either their right or left hand or forearm until they became aware of a very light, warm, relaxed feeling in that limb. They were then told to permit that limb to move across and rest on the abdomen and to let the relaxed, warm feeling in the fingers and hand to spread through the abdominal wall to the bowel which would also become relaxed. They were then advised that if they wished, they could permit the appropriate sphincters in the gastro-intestinal tract to contract gently and securely in a manner that would provide reassurance to them when they experienced the urge to defaecate.

This technique was practised regularly by the patients concerned and before long, all were able to exert far better bowel control than had previously been the case. What is important to bear in mind is that with a few exceptions where additional hypnotherapy was required, the procedure had depended on only average responsiveness to the induction of hypnosis and the accompanying relaxation effects.

## Hypnosis in Symptom Removal

A second area in which hypnosis can be applied clinically is in symptom removal (e.g. pain alleviation). Whereas relaxation can be achieved among subjects with only minimal degrees of hypnotisability, with symptom removal, a greater degree of hypnotisability has to be established in order to achieve the required responses, although this may not be the only factor, nor necessarily the most important. There again appears the question as to what extent symptoms should actually be removed - symptoms can reflect the degree of severity of a condition and hence should not be removed totally. It is probably more realistic therefore, to consider alleviating or reducing the severity of symptoms until one is certain that the condition generating such symptoms is itself resolved rather than removing such symptoms totally at too early a stage in the treatment. Such symptoms would provide a measure of the progress made in treating the underlying causes of the condition itself, especially if such a condition were identified as being psychogenic in origin.

The issue of symptom-removal would appear to be complicated and influenced by several factors. Schneck (1965) suggests that those symptoms necessary for the maintenance of psychological equilibrium will not be eliminated with ease, regardless of how neurotic that equilibrium might be.

Maher-Loughnan (1976) comments that many patients, from the start, press for symptoms to be treated directly in the cause of psychosomatic conditions. If tension is in part a contributory factor in symptom manifestation, then, as each therapeutic session takes the patient into deeper relaxation so physical and mental tensions are released, with the result that some symptom relief may occur early on in the treatment programme. Nevertheless, Maher-Loughnan (ibid.) considers it unwise to mention somatic disturbances too early on in hypnotherapy until a time comes when there is unequivocal evidence that symptoms are beginning to remit.

Early in treatment, possibly during the first or second session of hypnosis, patients may be asked quite simply whether they know the reasons behind their 'problems'. We have experienced, like others such as Hamson (1974), situations where, after a predictable pause, patients pressage their answers with expressions of dismay, sorrow or incredulity, followed by an emotional release and outpouring of repressed traumatic events that preceded the onset of their illness condition.

The period during which treatment involving relaxation, tension-reduction, possibly ego strengthening and subsequent relief of symptoms can vary greatly. It can be influenced by many factors including the patient's age and sex, the duration of the symptoms and the motivational drive towards recovery. In the latter instance, Mellett (1973) considers this to be probably the most important issue determining whether this leads to either partial or complete remission of symptoms. Thus, the time scale from the start of hypnotherapy to the moment at which symptoms begin to diminish varies for each patient, usually ranging between one to four months. Among older patients (60-65 years plus), this time scale may be appreciably longer.

In view of these effects, it is possible that many patients are able to adapt to the concept and the feeling of incipient relief *before* radical changes occur - they feel secure precisely because their ego defences are not under direct threat. Probably for this reason, it is rare for any but the more superficial and trivial of disorders to remit to any noticeable degree at the beginning of hypnotherapy.

Thus, the most likely approach to adopt when symptoms begin to disappear would be for the therapists to focus on them under hypnosis. The implication made to the patient would be that now that the symptom (specified by name) has started to go, the realisation of this will further accelarate its departure. The wording is deliberately kept fluid and permissive, not *directing* the patient but rather *suggesting* to the patient what it is they are *allowing* to happen.

A word of warning should be given at this point. Adopting a cavalier attitude towards symptom removal is ill-advised. It is important to establish if the condition being dealt with is entirely psychosomatic in origin and whether any of its symptoms, are organically based. For example, low back pain could be psychogenic or due to some specific physical trauma. Alternatively, such pain may be responsible for a secondary psychosomatic condition, such as a severe anxiety state.

In some instances, it may be that the existence of symptoms are essential to the patient's well-being, through some sub-conscious conflict. In such circumstances, the therapist might exercise an approach involving distorted sensory perceptions such as numbness or a tingling sensation to replace or mark the more discomforting symptoms including pain. The option is clearly with the patient to omit the practice or engage in it sparingly, according to his psychological/physiological needs or preference.

An appreciation of whether a condition is psychogenic in origin is often dependent on information elicited during the initial consultation, feedback from the patient's physician and, as a more conclusive exercise, by the use of hypnoanalysis.

Many clinical reports have recorded the use of hypnosis in the amelioration of almost any symptom that might manifest. It has also been used successfully in conjunction with other medical procedures e.g. in childbirth, analgesic and anaesthetic effects. Symptom remission may be attributable to just the state of relaxation, to enhanced confidence and placebo response, or possibly to perceptual distortion. In some instances e.g. gastro-intestinal conditions or bronchospasm might be adequately relieved by relaxation alone without the need for deeper hypnosis. In the reduction of pain (For techniques in pain control, see Chapter 6 ) due to organic disease, the ability of patients to distort perception and dissociate symptoms appears more advantageous. Obviously, there exists considerable room for development of appropriate experimental protocols in this clinical area in order to provide more accurate information.

## Hypnotherapy and hypnoanalysis in the treatment of psychosomatic and psychologically related conditions

Apart from endeavouring to reduce symptoms which manifest in psychosomatic conditions, the other prime requisite in treatment concerns the use of hypnosis combined with psychotherapy and analysis. Clear descriptions of the techniques used are elusive, primarily because of the variety of approaches included in the practice of psychotherapy and psychoanalysis.

Possibly because of concern as to the effectiveness and appropriateness of symptom removal by hypnosis, more attention has been given in recent years to developing hypnotherapy in order to resolve physical conditions due to psychogenic origins. The principle of such an approach suggests that by identifying the underlying psychological factors and assisting the patient to resolve these, the reduction of symptoms will begin to take place accordingly. We have frequently employed this approach with a considerable measure of success, the techniques being to use hypnosis as part of the psychotherapy and counselling sessions. As a form of positive reinforcement the patients tend to find that, as they resolve the psychological issues, some of which may have been repressed over a long-term period, the symptoms associated with the condition reduce, thereby enhancing the beneficial effects, both physically and psychologically.

In planning a programme for those being treated for psychosomatic conditions by hypnosis, a series of six appointments is appropriate, starting with an initial consultation in order to obtain a full case history and allowing for physical examination, should that be considered necessary. Sessions would tend to be of one hour's duration, at weekly intervals to begin with, then spaced to fortnightly intervals as the programme develops; a possible timetable would be as follows:

Week 1   Initial consultation (including tests for hypnotic susceptibility if appropriate) and hypnotic induction.
Week 2   Hypnoanalysis commences accompanied by ego strengthening.
Week 3   Hypnoanalysis continued and ego strengthening and hypnotherapy reinforced.
Weeks 4-6 Hypnotherapy reinforced as necessary.

Additional sessions can be included beyond week 6 if required although by that time, the patient may, during the course of hypnotherapy, have developed with the therapist's guidance, his own style of self-hypnosis. He can apply this on himself on a daily basis from around weeks 3 to 5 and as a means of reinforcing the sessions with the therapist. Follow-up during the course of four to twelve months following the initial sessions is of vital importance with these patients. It provides a link during the time that the person concerned adjusts to his new health patterns and minimises the risk of relapse.

By adopting the above programme or a similar regime, the incidence of relapses is low; Hill (1976) suggests a figure averaging less than four per cent. If and when they do occur, they can be more effectively handled then, than during the original consultations when the problem was dealt with from first principles. In the majority of such cases, reinforcement of previous hypnotherapy, including ego strengthening, is sufficient to overcome any threats the patient may suffer; rarely is there any need to repeat the full course, unless a new, major problem has arisen which the patient has had difficulty in coping with e.g. a bereavement or some other life crisis.

In focussing more closely on the main consultation programme, hypnoanalysis is considered an essential element in therapy. One tends to assume that, if dealing with conditions which are psychogenic, there always remains the possibility of some psychological and emotive element nurturing the presenting symptoms. Frequently, the patient may actually recognise the nature of the psychological cause, or at least be able to identify an event likely to be associated with the first signs of the problem. Nevertheless, it is essential to regress that person back to that episode in order to ensure that all the relevant details are accounted for within their conscious mind, and that no repressed events or episodes exist subconsciously. So as to effectively achieve this, age regression techniques can be applied when, following induction, deepening and establishing the ideo-motor response (IMR), the therapist takes the patient back over the years, identifying through the IMR, those ages at which some factor relating to the problem occurred (See Chapter 3).

When those ages/dates are identified, then at a subsequent session, the therapist can regress the patient back to that event and let him recall, relive or re-experience the episode; in so doing, clearer details of that episode may be brought into focus and frequently include facts which have been repressed or simply forgotten, but which may yet have had a direct bearing upon the problem.

By following this analytical approach with hypnotherapy, the point to emphasise to the patient is that such an event or episode need no longer preoccupy his mind, neither consciously nor sub-consciously. Recognition of these precipitating episodes as the likely precursor to their problems is very often the first stage of symptom removal, which, with additional therapy, including ego strengthening, can be observed to benefit the patient over subsequent weeks. Also, as mentioned previously, the patient's improved ability to relax, especially following release of emotional tension during hypnoanalysis, accentuates those beneficial effects.

The inclusion of ego-strengthening techniques in the therapy programme is essential on two counts:

1) it provides the patient with a 'target', namely how he would like to be and to feel;
2) by reinforcement through suggestion put to the patient by the therapist, the former comes to terms with the fact that he can and is feeling better and is adapting progressively to a new status quo, health-wise.

For this reason, ego strengthening can be introduced fairly early on in treatment, even in conjunction with analysis. Clinical observations have shown that ego-strengthening approaches can bring about benefit, in some cases even before hypnoanalysis has identified the repressed psychological agent underlying the actual conditions with which the patient has been referred. Futhermore, the ego strengthening is easily applied in post-hypnotic suggestions and can be drawn upon by the patient during his own sessions of self-hypnosis, between consultations.

This regime has been found to be easy to apply and rewarding in 75-80% of sufferers who become relieved of their disorders, thereby making an important contribution to the treatment of psychosomatic conditions.

## Contra-indications to hypnoanalysis and hynotherapy psychologically related problems

There do exist certain contra-indications to the regime of hypnoanalysis and therapy in treating psychosomatic conditions and hence some emphasis must be placed upon information gleaned from the patient's case history.

On the physical side, any indications of a cardio-vascular condition must be viewed with caution, as there could be an unpredictable outcome of the patient's responses under hypnosis. If there was a re-experiencing of a traumatic epiode which had occurred years previously, and which had become repressed, then, under such circumstances, the physiological responses to that stressful re-enactment could prove to be a risk to a coronary-prone subject. Similarly, hyperventilation, though by no means a contra-indication, can prove a physiological barrier to effective hypnosis, particularly if the state is undiagnosed and therefore, not corrected.

With respect to the latter, almost without exception, everyone will increase their minute-volume during entry into hypnosis. This is achieved by deeper breathing, faster respiration rate or possibly both. Once hypnosis is established e.g. by the deepening stage or beyond, the minute-volume decreases and the partial pressure of carbon dioxide [$Pa(CO_2)$] in the lungs rises again. Nevertheless, involuntary hyperventilation at rest with a resulting fall in [$Pa(CO_2)$] can be disturbing to hyperventilators whose [$Pa(CO_2)$] may already be fairly low.

With such individuals under hypnosis, fear or apprehension, possibly during some aspects of analysis, may accelarate respiration, resulting in a vicious circle to the extent that hypnosis is blocked entirely. Hartland (1971) maintains that this factor alone may account for 10 per cent of subjects considered to be 'unhypnotisable' by one therapist, but who can yet achieve a hypnotic state under the guidance of a different therapist; the latter person may be better able to allay the fears of the patient enough to minimise hyperventilation.

Conditions which illustrate this problem well are anxiety-based conditions, notably phobic states. Panic crises and hyperventilation are inexorably entwined, and hence a spontaneous fall of $CO_2$ during entry into hypnosis can be a very unpleasant and fearful experience. The problem can be overcome by teaching the patient preliminary exercises in hyperventilation and encouraging a slow, shallow breathing rhythm during hypnosis. When implemented, many phobic states can then be very effectively treated. On very few occasions, a patient may experience a self-induced, momentary episode of hyperventilation – appropriate strategies to deal with this are discussed in Chapter 3.

Other contra-indications may be the coexistence of endogenous depression or a psychosis. In the latter case, hypnoanalysis and hypnotherapy are generally precluded and should normally not be considered. The risk lies in that if hypnosis is applied, it might lead to the patient experiencing greater withdrawal from reality.

In the case of endogenous depression, such conditions are exceedingly difficult to deal with in hypnosis. More often than not, when depression exists as part of a psychosomatic condition, it can directly interfere with treatment of other (physical) symptoms and cause difficulties in hypnoanalysis. Often it is advisable to withhold treatment until the depression has been relieved by pharmaceutical means; there is then a chance that the burden of the somatic symptoms has been effectively diminished.

One of the limitations in dealing with cases of depression centres around the patients' poor motivational drives. Excluding depressives, most patients with psychosomatic disorders accept the idea of hypnosis with alacrity; provided that a two-pronged approach is adopted, incorporating a hypnoanalysis approach, employed to determine the 'cause' of the problem, together with the therapy/ego-strengthening approach, then a good hypnotic response can generally be guaranteed. Despite the controversial theories, minimal scientific evidence and difficulties in defining its nature, once having witnessed its effectiveness in treatment, one cannot readily lay it aside for want of research evidence and theoretical consistency.

The following case studies briefly illustrate the possible nature and causes of a selection of common psychologically related conditions.

### Anxiety States

Anxiety states can be caused by many factors, mainly those which inflict undue stress on the individual. Some states would seem to be physiologically-based, and others reactive. They are invariably a manifestation of the individual's inability to cope emotionally (and often physically) with a life situation. Certain personality traits would seem to be more vulnerable to the precipitation of anxiety states though other stressors, such as those provoked by the work situation, adverse personal relationships, emotional trauma, financial problems, and illness, can precipitate an anxiety state in the most resilient personality type. Whether the nature and causes of an anxiety state can be rationalised or not, the fact is that the anxiety is very real to the individual.

Most people suffer such states throughout the course of their lives and can usually cope with them quite effectively, without any professional help. Frequently, the state is resolved by the remission of its cause. It is when the anxiety determines the quality of the individual's life, often causing distress, emotional trauma and, frequently, physical malaise, that the problem is difficult to resolve without some professional help. There are many approaches to the treatment of anxiety states, including counselling, psychotherapy, relaxation therapy, drug therapy, and often a combination of these. Hypnotherapy can be a very effective adjunct to any of these therapies and has often been applied on its own, with significant success.

### Case Study 1

Carol, aged 28, was referred by her doctor, following treatment for cancer of the thyroid. Although the cancer condition had by all accounts been successfully overcome nearly a year earlier, she was continuing to experience, on a regular basis, the same kind of symptoms as existed when the condition was established. The symptoms involved a burning sensation in the neck, accompanied by spasms of breathing difficulty. The duration of the symptoms ranged from 4-6 days and occurred approximately every 18-24 days. She was having regular follow-up sessions with the consultant who had treated the condition and, despite the symptoms, there was no clinical evidence to suggest a recurrence.

At the time of her first hypnotherapy consultation, Carol was getting over a period of such symptoms. The period from which the condition was first recognised, through diagnosis and treatment, and the post-treatment period, was discussed. She was asked whether or not she felt that the condition still genuinely existed, or whether there might be other reasons for the appearance of the symptoms and her anxiety over this. She felt, in her own mind, that there was a possibility of recurrence but could not understand why.

It was agreed that hypnotherapy might be an appropriate of way of investigating what the problem might be, bearing in mind that there was no physical evidence to indicate a recurrence or metastases. Her other concern was that, whilst wanting help, she was of the opinion that she could not be hypnotised. It was therefore, decided to attempt an induction and, if successful, a deepening routine to verify her assertion. She proved to be a very susceptible subject and, in fact, was reluctant to leave the hypnotic state.

The second session took place a few days later. Induction and deepening were established, followed by an ideo-motor response (IMR). When questionned as to whether the symptoms stemmed from some experience before, during or after treatment for the thyroid cancer, though she could not locate an exact point in time, she responded affirmatively. A full age regression was then conducted to establish whether any other factors may have contributed to the condition prior to its diagnosis. The only response indicated by the raising of her index finger, was the period around treatment.

On focussing on that period, during the same session, it was found that a possible underlying cause of both the anxiety and recurrent symptom manifestation, centred on events shortly after treatment, including surgery. Working on the basis that there existed a strong psychological cause, ego strengthening was conducted, which suggested to Carol that the symptom effects would progressively diminish and disappear altogether. Should the symptoms continue to appear any time between our sessions, then she would find a quiet place on her own, and by letting herself progressively relax, allow herself to "breathe evenly and regularly, and become more and more relaxed". The IMR link was then 'broken' and the session concluded.

The third session took place a week later. Carol had not experience any of the symptoms since the last session although her underlying anxiety still existed. Regression, under hypnosis, back to the post-operative period ten months earlier, elicited no significant response for about five minutes. Further suggestion that she was returning to that period of time, emphasising the month and year, resulted in Carol showing obvious signs of agitation and distress, and she then began to cry. Encouraged to speak as freely as she wished, she started describing the hospital ward she was taken to after the operation. She reported that she was now starting to re-experience a discomfort around her neck that she had experienced then. The consultant was by her bedside quietly telling her about the success of the operation and informing her that she would be feeling a discomfort (as she was feeling at that moment). He also told her that hopefully "no rogue cancer cells had escaped into the system".

At this point, she was asked her whether she had remembered this episode before to which she replied in the negative, expressing her fears that there might still be some "rogue cells" in her bloodstream which could cause a recurrence of cancer, either back in the thyroid region or possibly in some other part of her body. It was suggested to her that the consultant had merely made a comment about a possibility of this happening and that, by all accounts, no such cells existed in her anymore. A positive attitude towards herself and the success of the operation was suggested, and having made sure that she was now calm and relaxed, she was brought back to the present time.

Following termination of hypnosis, Carol explained that for a few days following surgery, she had experienced considerable discomfort which included difficulty in swallowing and breathing. She recalled the consultant's regular visits but had no conscious recollection of the comments she recalled under hypnosis.

Carol attended two more sessions over the following month. She admitted feeling less anxious although she still remained somewhat apprehensive that the symptoms might recur. During these two sessions, attempts were made to establish, under hypnosis, the possibility of other psychogenic factors influencing the anxiety and symptoms but nothing was apparent. As suggested earlier on in treatment, once the traumatic episode responsible for the precipitation of the symptoms was revealed by Carol, the symptoms would remit. Positive reinforcement to the effect that she was free of the original condition, as indicated by medical tests, proved beneficial and reassuring to her. Later, recognisisng that the symptoms themselves were no longer apparent, the accompanying anxiety also reduced and eventually disappeared.

Although the condition was resolved and three years have elapsed since Carol was seen, with no reported further recurrence, the reason for the timing and duration of the symptom episodes was never conclusively resolved. One might speculate that the symptom onset related to some other external stressor e.g. work problems, or possibly, followed a cyclical pattern based upon the body's physiology and emotional responses to these. Regardless of such possible reasons, this element of the problem would not apparently have had any direct effect on the mode of treatment given.

## *Asthma*

It is not uncommon for clients referred to health care professionals for one condition to also be suffering from asthma; Examples of these are stutterers and clients with voice disorders. Most of these clients are likely to be under medication depending on the severity of their problem. Very often the asthma and the condition for which they have been referred are related and share the same underlying cause. Dealing with one condition and not the other may be counter productive.

It is generally accepted that whereas mild and moderate asthmatics may be helped by hypnotherapy, the technique should not be used with acute asthmatics nor during an attack; a preferable strategy being drug therapy. The psychogenic element of asthma has been well documented. It is in helping the client to cope with stress and preventing an asthma attack that hypnotherapy can be of greatest value.

*Case Study 2*

Naomi was an eight year old girl, the second in a family of three others. Most of the time she had no respiratory problems and when she had, it was well-controlled with 'Intal'. Her spinhaler went wherever she did. On a few occasions her attacks had been very severe and she had to be hospitalised. She seemed to be allergic to pollen and a few other agents but she was also very sensitive to her parents' constant marital rows. A child with an amiable disposition, she entered a trance quite readily and was taught relaxation and self-hypnosis. Great care was taken not to create an imaginary environment which she would be allergic to such as a garden, when inducing relaxation. During hypnosis, she was encouraged to put her hand on her chest and relax. She said she liked the beach so she was encouraged to imagine herself on a beach watching a little sailing boat bobbing up and down on a very calm sea. She was asked to breathe in and out rhythmically as the boat gently danced up and down. She was told that she could practise this whenever she felt she was getting stressed. She would think of her breathing 'tubes' and 'tell' them to open to allow air to go in and out through them easily and in a relaxed way. If however, she found herself in an attack, she should use her spinhaler immediately. Her parents witnessed all the sessions and this advice was stressed to them. Both heavy smokers, they were advised to give up the habit or confine their smoking to a certain part of the house which Naomi was unlikely to use. After six sessions, Naomi seemed to have learned how to relax. Subsequent enquiries indicated that Naomi did occasionally practise relaxation and that she only occasionally used the spinhaler. The advantages of employing hypnotherapy as an adjunct to (or instead of) drug therapy has been well documented but it must not be thought that hypnotherapy on its own can resolve all cases of asthma and this is primarily a medical condition which should not be treated without medical supervision.

## Migraine

Sometimes referred to as 'tension headaches', there would seem to be no doubt that migraine has both an organic and psychogenic etiology. Many migraine sufferers report that drug therapy does not help and at best, only very negligibly reduces the discomfort.

This could be because the client does not actually suffer from migraine but his headaches have been misdiagnosed as such. His headaches may indeed be solely due to severe tense states. They may, on occasions be due to other pathologies such as a brain tumour, vascular conditions, etc.. It is for this reason that it is important for the hypnotherapist to seek medical clearance from the client's doctor before any hypnotherapy is started.

Migraine is often a very debilitating condition which can last for a short period of time or even days. There would seem to be different types of migraine. Sufferers of one type may not get prior warning of an impending attack and others might. The latter are therefore able to take some steps to prepare themselves or take medication. The symptoms can range from a headache to more severe symptoms such as a complete hemiplegia and dysphasic-type loss of speech.

*Case Study 3*

Tracey was a student of ours who attended a demonstration of hypnosis one of us gave after her final examinations. The demonstrator was not aware that she was a migraine sufferer. She volunteered to be one of the subjects to be induced into a light trance. It was noticed as she was going into hypnosis that she was resisting somewhat and she was exhibiting a cataleptic eye-flutter which lasted longer than expected. She was reassured that she could close her eyes if she so wished and that nothing unpleasant would happen to her. The demonstration over, she was asked for her feelings about the experience and she agreed that she had volunteered because she wanted to experience hypnosis as she was contemplating this form of therapy for her migraine; drug therapy had not been helpful, particularly since she rarely had pre-warning of an attack. She had in fact hesitated because it had been a new experience for her and she had shared a common suspicion about the alleged dangers of hypnosis.

Having gone through it, she acknowledged that once she had settled down, she had enjoyed it. She asked for hypnotherapy which was agreed upon, provided medical clearance was provided by her doctor; this he did. Being close to end of term and her return home being imminent, there was not much time and only two further sessions were possible. However, she responded well in the first session but she had already said that she did not want to experience arm levitation as this might be too much like the kind of numb feeling she used to get as a migraine attack started. In fact, in its most severe form she would experience hemiplegia on the right side and, frequently, total loss of speech.

Tracey learned auto-hypnosis very quickly. She was advised to practise this, particularly before stressful situations (such as going for job interviews). An appropriate ego-strengthening routine was conducted on both sessions.

Several months later, Tracey telephoned to enquire about our hypnosis workshops as she wanted to attend. She reported she had not had a migraine attack since she last saw me. Yet a few months later, she attended the workshop and again reported that she practised auto-hypnosis when she felt she needed to and that she had not had any further attacks. She had also told her doctor that she did not feel she needed any further medication and he obliged.

## Insomnia

### Case Study 4

John, a 68 year old client, was referred for psychotherapy, presenting with insomnia and occasional trembling. At the time of referral, his wife was recovering from surgery for cancer and because of her weakened state, was limited in what she could do. The responsibility for looking after her and maintaining the home thus fell upon John's shoulders.

During the first consultation, John described many of the characteristic symptoms of the 'insomnia'. He maintained that he was only sleeping about two hours each night. On waking he would try to go back to sleep, but ultimately would get up and pace around the house. Gradually, he began to fear going to bed the next night in case he would be unable to sleep. He also imagined that if this state of affairs was to continue, he would suffer mental harm, become more anxious and be unable to cope with his everyday routines.

The first and foremost task in treating insomnia is to try and discover the cause. In John's case, there existed evidence of physical tension, possibly reflecting his anxiety regarding his symptoms. In the first session involving hypnosis, induction and progressive relaxation was carried out, followed by deepening. The deepening technique involved John imagining that he was walking down the length of a terraced garden which terminated at the edge of a lake. As he imagined himself walking and descending from one terrace to the next, so his 'relaxed' state would deepen and all physical tension would be released by the time he arrived at the water's edge. Once deepening was achieved, the ideo-motor response was induced, enabling him to respond to questions or indicate what was happening without the need to think consciously nor verbalise.

During the next two consultations, hypnoanalysis was conducted. This involved age regression in order to determine whether a particular episode or series of events had precipitated the problem, and if so, when. In John's case, the significant factor was learning of his wife's cancer. Further analysis revealed that his anxiety and trembling were most closely allied to this, the insomnia being a secondary effect which in turn was developing into a habit. At the same time that analysis was being carried out, ego-strengthening techniques were being applied in order to enable John to enjoy a more prolonged sleep pattern and, should he have woken up in the middle of the night or during the early hours of the morning, to be able to go back to sleep without too much difficulty. As part of the treatment, whilst under hypnosis, John re-enacted his previous night's experience which confirmed that while he had no difficulty in falling asleep on going to bed, he was only sleeping about two hours before awaking and remaining so most of the night apart from a short spell of sleep around dawn.

John attended for consultation on a weekly basis. During the first three weeks which focussed on hypnoanalysis with some ego strengthening, there was a slight improvement. Following the next three consultations (weeks 4 - 6) a greater improvement was found to occur resulting in John finally having a minimum of five hours sleep at night. This was due largely to anxiety reduction and use of visual imagery whilst under hypnosis during which John visualised himself lying in bed, "fully relaxed, less tense and anxious as gradually, drowsiness envelops you". Thereafter, he would find himself "falling into a natural sleep again ....... which will last undisturbed until your usual time for getting up in the morning".

Interestingly, the reduction in anxiety, as well as improving the sleep pattern, led to a more rapid reduction in the trembling spasms that John had experienced. Although John did not often exceed 5 - $5^1/_2$ hours sleep each night, two factors had to be considered. Firstly, because of his age, he probably required less sleep compared to a younger person at work. Secondly, because of his wife's condition and her occasional awakening during the night, he was very conscious of this and would awake to see if she was having difficulties.

The programme of therapy took six weeks. John was aware that, should it have been necessary to 'reinforce' the beneficial effects of the hypnotherapy, he could use auto-hypnosis or, if he wished to, he could contact us again.

## Bulimia Nervosa

### Case Study 5

Jane, 22, was referred from a local hospital and had shown symptoms of bulimia nervosa. She had just completed her second year examinations at University where she was studying biology. On coming home at the beginning of the summer vacation, her parents discovered by chance that she had the condition bulimia nervosa, a condition characterised by the subject purposely bringing up food she had recently eaten. She was hospitalised for a short time during which she was largely confined to bed with a nurse sitting with her after meals to ensure that Jane did not try to vomit. On being discharged, Jane appeared to cope and was looking forward to returning to college. Four weeks before commencing her final year studies, Jane's mother discovered that her daughter was once again exhibiting bulimia nervosa symptoms. This time, with the agreement of the hospial, it was suggested that Jane be referred for psychotherapy.

At the first consultation, some background to Jane's circumstances were made clear. She was the youngest of four children, the other three having left home and pursuing various occupations, two of them abroad. Jane's father was intending early retirement and because of marital problems, there was a likelihood of he and Jane's mother separating. Jane also implied that she was under pressure from her mother not to move from home once her university studies were completed.

Jane proved an excellent hypnosis subject. After the first two sessions, both within a week, she was able to attain medium depth hypnosis on hearing the therapist use a trigger word, established as a post-hypnotic suggestion. Deepening and the ideo-motor response were established on each occasion. The initial approach taken was to help her overcome the symptoms of bulimia nervosa, including the use of ego strengthening, whilst at the same time attempt to define the underlying cause of the condition. It was only through age regression and overcoming repression that the reason behind her problem was revealed. Some six years earlier, her mother had stated to Jane that she was just like her mother, and because of that, would very likely become overweight. Jane had no wish to be like her mother, neither physically nor emotionally. (Such were her mother's problems that she too consulted us shortly after Jane's condition was resolved).

Over a further four sessions (there being six in total), Jane was put through hypnotherapy involving body image, feelings of comfort after eating meals and being able to eat all her meals, which until recently she had not been doing. Motivation was not a problem for this patient. Her routine whilst at home was modified so that regular meals were eaten, but the main course being served on smaller plates. Within a four week period, the symptoms were eliminated and Jane was able to return to her studies which she completed successfully. Long term monitoring of Jane's progress indicated no further relapse.

## Conclusions

There is little doubt that hypnotherapy can help clients with psychosomatic and other psychologically-related problems. Equally so, the use of hypnotherapy for such conditions and by unqualified or untrained 'dabblers' can cause clients unnecessary and sometimes needless and harmful effects. It must also be pointed out that often hypnotherapy on its own may not be enough and other types of therapy must be employed, such as psychotherapy or even drug therapy. It would therefore, be not only irresponsible but also, unethical for a hypnotherapist who might be a competent hypnotist to attempt to deal with these conditions by hypnosis alone as he may not be qualified to recognise the need for other or adjunctive forms of therapy.

# CHAPTER 5
# Hypnotherapy for Communication Disorders

## Samuel Abudarham

The use of hypnosis for the treatment of disorders of oral human communication is not a recent development. However, early published work in this field was conducted by physicians or psychiatrists. This is not particularly surprising since speech therapy as a profession has only existed for half a century or so in the United Kingdom. Whereas there is evidence that speech therapists in this country were practising hypnosis for conditions such as stuttering and functional voice disorders, the first nationally-advertised, formal course on record for speech therapists and members of the Health Care professions was run in Birmingham by Abudarham and Hughes in July 1983. A few months later, a training course was offered in Scotland but this was for speech therapists only. Soon afterwards, the Scottish Society for the Practice of Hypnosis in Speech Therapy was founded and, following official sanction from the College of Speech Therapists (CST), the Society opened its membership to all speech therapists in Britain, changing its name by substituting "British" for "Scottish". By that time, hypnosis courses were being run for speech therapists by the National Hospitals College of Speech Sciences, in London.

The significance of this brief history lies in establishing the speech therapy profession's recognition that hypnosis was already being practised by some of its members and that hypnotherapy was a legitimate and effective adjunct to speech therapy. Speech therapists were thus the first of the Health Care professions, and to date the only ones, whose professional council acknowledged and approved of the practice. The CST even set up a working party in 1986, comprising a clinical psychologist, physician and three speech therapists (which included this author), whose remit was to propose guidelines for courses and standards for practice. This was a welcome development indeed and, somewhat untypically, the CST made a unilateral decision to give official sanction to a practice about which the medical profession had been very guarded. In its 1955 report, the BMA recommended that

> ".... the use of hypnotism in the treatment of physical and psychological disorders should be confined to persons subscribing to the recognised ethical code which governs the relation of doctor and patient. *This would not preclude its use by a suitably trained*

> *psychologist or **medical auxiliary** of whose competence the medical practitioner was personally satisfied, and who would carry out, under medical direction, the treatment of patients selected by the physician."* (My emphasis)

Whether the term 'medical auxiliary' in this recommendation covered speech therapists was not clear but the BMA recommended that such auxiliaries should only practise under the supervision of medically qualified practitioners. No recommendation was made that the 'supervising' medical practitioner had to have been trained in hypnotherapy himself. The next BMA report in 1986 omits mention of 'medical auxiliaries' and recommends that ".... the use of hypnotherapy should be restricted to medical practitioners, dentists and trained and qualified clinical psychologists" (p. 77), (whether the intention was that medical practitioners and dentists did not need to be 'trained and qualified' is not clear!) despite Dr. Gibson's evidence that hypnosis had ".... wide applications in .... and *speech therapy*"!

Despite all this, there is now a growing number of speech therapists who are using hypnosis to help clients with communication problems such as functional dysphonia and stuttering. Interestingly, the speech therapist had for years been dealing with psychiatrically-related conditions such as hysterical or functional dysphonias. Today, many work with patients with other psychiatric conditions such as schizophrenia, depression and senile dementia, who also have a communication problem.

## General considerations

Communication disorders can be caused by many factors which include environmental, psychological and organic. Many disorders of communication are extremely complex and the speech therapist requires an understanding of subjects such as linguistics, sociology, normal and clinical psychology, anatomy, physiology and neurology, in order to be competent to assess and treat them. Formulating the differential diagnosis is often not easy and requires a speech therapy professional skill and also an awareness of other professionals' roles. For example, a dysphonia could be organically caused by different types of vocal cord pathology e.g. vocal nodules, paralysis, etc., or could be entirely psychologically based as a result of stress and other emotional determiners. The differential diagnosis therefore, often depends on the speech therapist being able to make use of correct appraisal procedures some of which are beyond his expertise.

Almost invariably, for example, the diagnostic skills of an ENT specialist are required before the final differential diagnosis for a voice disorder can be made by the speech therapist. A correct diagnosis is an essential prerequisite for an appropriate management programme. In addition, a holistic approach must be taken, and in order to achieve this, the therapist must acquire other information to help him understand his client and his problems, and how the latter affects the client's life at all levels.

Anyone dealing with the treatment of communication disorders should follow standard procedures used in speech therapy of case history taking, appropriate and valid assessment of the particular communication problem, etc. when a client is referred, regardless of whether hypnotherapy is likely to be used or not. Furthermore, before and once the decision has been made to use hypnotherapy, some of the appraisal procedures mentioned in Chapter 2 should be followed, as appropriate, particularly those related to case history taking, testing the client's motivation and commitment, and preparation of the client.

Before any management strategy is employed, a careful process of rationalisation must take place which considers all known factors about the client and his condition, etc.. The strategy chosen must be tailor-made for the client's needs and circumstances.

Choosing a strategy such as hypnotherapy is therefore, not done lightly, nor in the absence of knowledge about the condition and whether, all things considered, hypnotherapy is likely to benefit the client. It would therefore, be unwise and unethical, for anyone without the necessary training in the nature, assessment and treatment of communication disorders to attempt to remediate such disorders, whether through hypnotherapy or otherwise.

## Brief literature review

The early published literature is equivocal about the benefits of hypnotherapy for communication problems. Van Riper (1973) admits that it is difficult to evaluate the literature concerning the use of hypnotherapy for stutterers. Abudarham and Hughes (1983) stated that "There is almost invariably a lack of information about the techniques used, type of stuttering dealt with and follow-up studies". Luchsinger and Arnold (1965) concluded that with regard to psychiatric aspects in stuttering therapy, hypnosis is only of help in "acute traumatic cases of stuttering" and it had not achieved "convincing or lasting results in chronic stutterers". They offer no detail about how patients were selected, types of stutter they suffered from, how long treatment lasted, hypnotherapy techniques employed, patients' hypnotisability, etc.. Van Riper (op. cit.) makes similar criticism about published work in this field. He also comments on the weakness of post hypnotic suggestion which does not prevent relapse.

There is some evidence that hypnotherapy is more effective when used with other traditional speech therapy techniques. Rousey (1961) acknowledged this and stated that hypnosis was likely not to be effective if the patient could not be deeply hypnotised. Hypnosis has been employed together with other techniques such as systematic desensitisation and Van Riper used it to induce relaxation while stutterers spoke.

Of course, hypnotherapy has not been used with stutterers only. Wilson (1979) briefly reports on studies conducted on the use of hypnosis as a "psychotherapeutic approach to control vocal abuse in children". Laquarte (1976) hypnotised 18 children (mean age of 6 years 8 months, the youngest being four and a half years) who had vocal nodules. One of the children was helped to analyse situations in which he shouted. The need to shout was then reduced and this resulted in a reduction of vocal abuse. Laquarte (ibid.)

reports impressive results. Initially, hypnosis was used to enhance the children's motivation. It was also employed, subsequently, to identify the causes of the children's tension. Of the fifteen children who completed the course, thirteen showed improvement in the appearance of their vocal apparatus, and the nodules disappeared or atrophied in seven of them.

Hypnotic treatment for speech dysfunction is likely to be most effective among children. There tends to be inconsistent findings, although, among those cases which fail to show improvement initially, a greater degree of success has resulted when hypnosis has been used in conjunction with other speech therapy techniques.

Hartland (1971) believes that a deep hypnotic state is preferable in the treatment of psychogenic speech dysfunction, in order for desensitisation techniques to be applied. Under such conditions, it is found that the patient can speak normally whilst completely calm and relaxed. By gradually reducing the depth of hypnosis, the therapist is then in a position to assist the patient in speaking without any speech dysfunction. Eventually, the normal speech pattern is extended to the waking state.

Because this chapter is aimed predominantly at speech therapists, I have decided that there is no need to describe the different types of communication disorders, nor to explain terminology. Furthermore, rather than itemise each condition and suggest how hypnotherapy might help each one, it will be more useful to explore some of the techniques used in hypnotherapy and provide examples, as appropriate, of communication disorders which may benefit from such techniques.

## The role of relaxation

Because most clients with psychologically-based communication problems suffer from undue tension which causes or exacerbates their communication problem, it is common speech therapy practice to use relaxation therapy. The objective of such therapy is to train clients to identify when they are tense and to help them develop techniques which will enable them to relax themselves independently from a therapist's supervision. Some clients find it very difficult to learn to relax on their own. It must be said however, that my own observations of the relaxation training given by some professionals have given me repeated impressions that sometimes the training given to clients is not adequate enough to help them develop such a skill. A proper programme can not be covered by a five minute session before the more direct treatment on the particular communication problem commences. Most clients have suffered tension for many years and are likely to be in that state for most of the day, every day of the week. To expect that they can suddenly learn to become invulnerable to the day's pressures and to 'switch on' to a relaxation mode at will and without intensive training, is totally unrealistic.

Another problem is that many clients find it difficult to achieve the deep relaxation which might be required, or to maintain a relaxed state throughout a treatment session. Many such clients relax better under hypnosis and can therefore often maintain an appropriate state of relaxation whilst under hypnosis for as long as is necessary within a treatment session. Perhaps one of the greatest advantages of a hypnotically-induced relaxation state is that after the first session, and in response to a previously given post-hypnotic suggestion, a client can enter a state of relaxation in response to a trigger word or other signal from the therapist, within seconds. Time has therefore, not got to be wasted going through an otherwise lengthy routine.

The client can also be taught to relax when on his own through various means such as auto-hypnosis and techniques such as Stein's (1963) 'clenched fist'. This latter technique is taught to the client whilst under hypnosis. A post-hypnotic suggestion is given to the client that whenever he feels tense and anxious, he should clench the fist (a common suggestion refers to the fist of the preferred hand). By doing this, it is suggested to the client that he will be able to 'transfer' and dissipate all the tension and anxiety that he feels. The dissipation takes place symbolically when the client opens his fist and 'drops' the tension out of his hand. The client is instructed that after he has done this he should take three or four gentle and relaxed breaths to help him compose and calm himself. This method often produces quick and effective release from tension. It is also particularly helpful because clients such as stutterers can not always predict when they are going to get tense and if they do so they may not have the time or opportunity for a brief session of auto-hypnosis.

*Case Study 1*

A case in point was Robin, a moderate stutterer, who had prepared a lecture which he had to give to the directors of the firm he was working for. He reported he had prepared every detail to the last 'T' and felt very confident, so much so that he was encouraging a colleague of his who was speaking first and was giving her reassurance that she would do well. When his time came he started off very confidently but a few minutes into his lecture, he fell to pieces and struggled to use all the techniques he had been taught during one of our sessions, in preparation for this big day.

Whereas the fist is probably the most convenient focus for the 'transfer' of tension, any other motor behaviour could serve the same purpose though it should not be one which is so conspicuous that it is likely to make the client more self-conscious. A variation of this method could include a post-hypnotic suggestion that on clenching the fist of the other hand, calmness will be restored, etc..

One should point out that many communication problems may have both strong organic and psychological components. There is still some misconception, for example, that all stutters are entirely psychogenic; this is of course not so and recent research has confirmed that there are types of stutters which are predominantly organically determined though it is not denied that 'organic' stutters may be accompanied, and exacerbated by psychological factors. There are other disorders which may be entirely organically determined, such as dysphonias caused by damage to the vocal chords or nerves supplying them, dysarthria, dyspraxia, laryngectomy etc., which may also be exacerbated by the client's anxiety and self-consciousness. These too, may often benefit from relaxation.

Ewing (1985) used hypnotherapy to help neurologically impaired patients with a high stress factor and/or Cardiac Type 'A' personalities to relax and improve their sleeping patterns. She reports on one such aphasic patient and states that, not only was he able after training to use auto-hypnosis successfully, but he was beginning to take better control of his life, cope better with stress, and, "after relaxation, he exhibits far less literal and verbal paraphasic errors"; the patient was also aware of his improved fluency. I would propose that it was more likely that his fluency improved not so much because hypnosis helped reduce 'paraphasic' errors but those speech errors caused by the anxiety and tension these patients suffer from because of their communicative difficulties. Nevertheless, it is clear that hypnotherapy can enhance such patients' speech and fluency. Hypnotherapy has also been used to motivate aphasic patients to strive towards working hard to improve their speech and language with therapy.

It is appropriate at this point, to emphasise that medical approval must be sought and obtained before hypnotherapy is considered for cardiac or neurologically impaired patients.

## Identifying causal and associated factors

It is sometimes important to identify causal factors underlying communication problems. Some precipitating factors could also continue to contribute to and maintain the client's problem. It may be that such factors need remediation themselves before the core problem can be treated. A typical example is the functional (or as once popularly referred to, 'hysterical') dysphonic client whose problem may be entirely psychologically determined and maintained. Dunnet and Williams (1988) state that patients with this problem do not respond to traditional voice therapy and require what could be a slow and long counselling process in order to discover the cause of the disorder.

Many clients find it very difficult to recall when a problem started and even more difficult to establish what might have caused it. It could well be that the client has suppressed an experience which was responsible for the problem. Such suppression itself may in fact underly the perpetuation of the problem.

Endeavouring to establish a cause and effect relationship for all communication disorders, is normal practice for speech therapists as a knowledge of an etiology may be crucial in determining a differential diagnosis. Furthermore some etiological factors may be maintaining and/or contributing to the problem. If this is the case, they may have to be dealt with as well. Investigation of possible causal and maintaining factors is usually done through verbal interview and during the counselling exercise. On occasions, and not under hypnosis, clients may find themselves recalling and revealing some painful experiences which are often related in distress.

The speech therapist is trained to cope with such situations. Very often, the client expresses surprise that he has confided in the therapist when at the beginning of the session he had had no intention of doing so. And yet, as the session proceeds and, presumably as a therapeutic relationship develops, the client feels ready and an urge to 'offload' his most private secrets. This situation is not very different to the one a client may find himself in when revealing his 'private' thoughts under hypnosis. There are those however, who will argue that helping the client to recall such experiences under hypnosis is not the same and that only those with appropriate training in psychiatry or clinical psychology should employ such techniques. I find some sympathy with this proposal particularly if the technique being used is regression analysis.

Some clients however, are aware at a conscious level of the etiology behind their problem and whereas they may not wish to reveal it 'cold', may be happier to do so under a hypnotically-induced relaxed state and without the necessity for regression analysis. If the therapist feels it is important to identify the etiology of the problem under hypnosis (though not through regression analysis) it should be discussed with the client and prior approval sought.

I am of course not denying the potential benefit of regression analysis when dealing with clients with psychologically-based communication disorders, but I am advocating that those who wish to practise it should have received appropriate training, particularly in dealing with any ensuing trauma. It is interesting to note that Lockhart and Robertson (1977) could not identify any one early traumatic experience, as revealed through regression analysis, which they felt convincingly explained the cause of their patients' stutter. They also concluded that the results of their study suggested that "a single traumatic experience is not of aetiological significance in the development of the stuttering syndrome." They do however, propose that age regression might be of value "as an anxiety releasing mechanism where repressed trauma exist as a result of .... experiences related to the stammer." On the other hand, Van Riper (op. cit.) warns that sometimes, clients may make up an experience which could explain the cause of a problem or which they think the therapist wishes to hear. The exercise may therefore, not yield reliable results.

## Ego strengthening

Most communication problems, whether organic or entirely psychologically based, are exacerbated by the client's anxiety about his poor communication skills and his lack of confidence in situations which require verbal interaction. It is for this reason that ego-strengthening routines may benefit such clients but in order for these to be effective, the therapist needs to have a good knowledge of the exact nature of these situations, the client's feelings in such situations, and the strategies he uses to avoid or survive them. This is particularly relevant to stutterers.

An ego-strengthening programme can complement a programme of desensitisation which could be conducted under hypnosis. Once a well structured hierarchy of anxiety-producing events related to communication situations has been established between the therapist and client, the latter can be asked to imagine each in turn, under hypnosis, starting from the mildest, and gradually working through to the severest. It is often useful to act out a situation whilst the client is under hypnosis, the therapist taking the role of the interlocutor imagined by the client and the latter asked to speak to the therapist who would in turn maintain or lead the conversation. This exercise can be preceded by discussion whilst the client is awake about the situation to be role-played, the roles to be taken by the therapist and client, and anything else which may make the role-play as realistic as possible. The exercise should also be preceded by appropriate relaxation-inducing and ego-strengthening techniques.

Once the whole graded programme is completed 'imaginally', it can then be extended to 'in vivo' (actual) situations. These should again be graded according to the client's hierarchy of anxiety levels predicted for each situation; each 'in vivo' step being preceded by appropriate 'ego strengthening'. The programme can then be effected in the form of assignments conducted independently by the client, in a group of other clients with similar communication problems, or in the presence of the therapist, depending on whether any one of these is thought to be a criterion in the grading structure. Feedback and discussion on the client's performance and his feelings should follow, if possible, immediately after each assignment.

During all this time, the client could be helped to modify any negative attitudes he might have and which might have an adverse effect on his progress. Similarly, he can be trained to become more assertive in difficult situations particularly on important events in his life such as examination vivas, interviews for new jobs, giving important talks or lectures, etc.

## Auto-hypnosis

It is always my principle to train clients in auto-hypnosis so that they can become independent 'self-healers'. There is usually a lot of variation in one's life; on some days one can feel very vulnerable and unable to cope with the slightest pressure and on others one can feel impervious to life's stresses. Clients can therefore not always predict how the day is going to turn out. Auto-hypnosis is often very effective in motivating a client or even restoring shattered confidence.

It ought to be emphasised that not all clients can learn auto-hypnosis and those who do may need more than one training session. The therapist needs to give the client adequate time to develop such a skill, and allow him an opportunity to demonstrate how he practises self-hypnosis so that the therapist can confirm that the skill has been acquired, and if not, give the client advice on how best to do so. The therapist should also monitor the client's attempts away from the consulting room by requiring the client to report on the success or otherwise of such attempts.

## Case Study 2

David was a thirty year old confirmed, moderate stutterer. He had received 'conventional' speech therapy as an adult and was reasonably pleased with the results. He had been taught to use prolonged speech. An intelligent, professional person who needed to interact continuously with his clients, he initially approached me because he wanted experience in speaking to large groups and he felt he could at the same time offer the benefit of his experiences to my speech therapy students. He gave a very fluently delivered talk and, had the students not been told in advance, many would not have realised that he was a stutterer. However, immediately after the talk, whilst talking casually to me and having 'dropped his guard', his dysfluency returned. He reported that even though he had been very fluent, he had been very anxious before the talk and asked if I could help. After some discussion, I suggested that in his case, hypnosis might help.

A useful induction technique employed with him, required him to close his eyes and imagine a beautifully polished cartwheel. At the bottom of the wheel was a rose bud and as the cart wheel started rotating slowly, David had to follow the rose bud with his 'gaze'. As the bud went up, so he had to breathe in and as it started coming down, he had to breathe out. This technique seemed to help him establish a balanced breathing rhythm which helped him to relax. It was suggested that as he followed the circular path of the bud, so he would relax deeper and deeper until he entered a medium trance.

Under hypnosis, his fluency improved markedly and on occasions he was entirely fluent. It was clear that he resented his stutter tremendously. During one session, it was suggested to him that he could imagine that he could trap his stutter in a securely fastened steel box. He was then to imagine he was on a boat which he would row to the deepest part of a lake and he would then proceed to sink his 'stutter'.

During discussion in a wake state, he said he had enjoyed doing this and that he had felt a sense of hatred for the stutter which turned into a deep exhileration when he got rid of it. At a subsequent session, he was asked if he wanted to retrieve the stutter and find a deeper place to sink it into. He refused, preferring to leave it where it was.

The hypnotherapy programme included ego strengthening and training in auto-hypnosis. After several sessions, I was a little concerned that sometimes, post-session, he began to stutter again. I called his attention to this and he said he had not quite noticed. He admitted he still caught himself stuttering on occasions but felt that hypnosis had helped him in not worrying too much if he did and that he found auto-hypnosis very useful before any feared speaking situation.

## Modifying behaviour and learning new strategies

Particularly in clients with psychologically-based communication problems, associated maladaptive behaviour patterns often reflecting an underlying anxiety neurosis, often form part of the 'syndrome'. Van Riper (op. cit.)

successfully used hypnosis to help stutterers "react more appropriately to fear or experience of their stuttering." For example, a stutterer may have developed a nervous tic which could accompany every speech act; he may go into facial grimaces or contortions which he might think are necessary to release sounds or words he blocks on.

These behaviour patterns can be dealt with under hypnotherapy. Van Riper (op. cit.) reports that the greatest success of hypnosis was in helping stutterers unlearn instrumental behaviours, such as pre-speech head jerks, much quicker than expected through other means. Traditional speech therapy techniques can sometimes be learned best under hypnosis. Van Riper (op. cit.) employed hypnosis to train his clients to use cancellations and pullout techniques. He reported however, that many clients overused these strategies and though their stuttering decreased, their fluency was affected by the excessive use of the strategies they had learned. Lockhart and Robertson (op. cit.) successfully found that hypnotherapy on its own helped a group of 'mild' stutterers whose etiology was thought to be predominantly psychogenic. However, with a group of more severe stutterers who exhibited blocking behaviour and much accompanying tension, and whose etiology was thought to be mainly organic, they used both hypnotherapy and block control techniques. Their patients' awareness of tactile feedback was enhanced under hypnosis and suggestions were given to help the patients associate block control with confidence and relaxation. They also used the hypnotherapy to help maintain and stabilise their patients' progress.

Under hypnosis a client with a stutter or functional dysphonia may be able to speak fluently and clearly. Even aphonic patients with no organic vocal pathology might be able to phonate under hypnosis. Many of the clients who achieve enhanced fluency or phonation under hypnosis may relapse in the wake state even though post-hypnotic suggestion might have been given that they will speak fluently or clearly when they wake up. However, the experience itself could be a valuable aid in the recovery progress as the client may realise that he is capable of normal speech behaviour. One has to deal very carefully with this occurrence though as the client may not be able to handle being confronted with such evidence and he may find this very threatening. The use of audio-recordings to provide the client with evidence of his normal speech behaviour, albeit under hypnosis, should be considered very carefully and the client has to be prepared very well before he is faced with it.

During an ego-strengthening and post-hypnotic suggestion routine, it is often better not to refer to the client's communication problem under hypnosis but suggest feelings of calmness and relaxation. Thus, a functional dysphonic can be encouraged to feel his throat muscles and vocal cords relaxing before he starts to speak without the therapist suggesting that he will be able to speak clearly. Suggestions can also be made that he will feel confident, and progressively more comfortable. The same approach can be adopted for stutterers once the foci of their bodily tension have been identified so that they can be referred to during the ego-strengthening and post-hypnotic suggestion routine.

Van Riper (op. cit.) found that whereas fluency was obtained when the client was in a deep trance, only momentary fluency was obtained following appropriate post-hypnotic suggestion. Better, though still not long-lasting, results were obtained when without mentioning the stutter, clients were hypnotically induced into relaxation and asked to speak. Then post-hypnotic suggestions were made that the client would speak just as fluently when awake. Whereas the stuttering became markedly less severe and without accompanying anxiety, the effect did not last long.

Van Riper (op. cit.), himself a stutterer, acknowledges that hypnotherapy may have not worked for him because of lack of faith on his part, in the effectiveness of the technique. He concludes nevertheless, that little can be achieved under hypnosis which can not be achieved employing non-hypnotic techniques. It is difficult to evaluate his work with hypnotherapy because he does not give details of how long the training took. In my experience, much is often expected from a very short period of hypnotherapy (sometimes not more than six sessions) which is not expected from an equivalent or even longer period of training with more traditional techniques. It is no wonder in these cases that hypnotherapy does not benefit the client.

Lockhart and Robertson (op. cit.) saw their stutterers over a period ranging from 12-54 weeks though "on average fluency was stabilised by 30-40 weeks, the patients having been reviewed several times at monthly intervals."

Richter (1928) used hypnosis with his stutterers requiring them to repeat simple words fluently and then progressing to speaking sentences slowly and carefully until the stutter disappeared. He acknowledged however, that fluent speaking under hypnosis has to be done for some time. He found that post-hypnotic suggestions about not stuttering had to be preceded by adequate training in *fluent* speaking before they could be effective. Van Riper (op. cit.) invokes his own experience in support for his claim that "negative post-hypnotic suggestion that the person will *not* stutter seems to be not only unwise but dangerous."

## Associated problems

Very often the cause of a psychologically-based communication problem is responsible for other accompanying problems. Sometimes the communication problem will not resolve unless other problems are dealt with before, or simultaneously.

*Case Study 3*

Joyce was a 36 year old lady who had a severe functional dysphonia. In the course of treatment she told the therapist that she felt that most of her problems would resolve if she could reduce her weight substantially from the twelve stones she then weighed. Clearly, both her dysphonia and weight problem were related. She felt that because of her oversize she had lost her self-esteem and her husband had lost interest in her. She was sure that her relationship with her husband would improve if she could recover her pre-marital weight. She also agreed that her dysphonia might improve as well.

She had tried reducing weight several times before and had never succeeded. Her doctor had said there was nothing medically wrong with her and she felt she over-ate because of anxiety. She agreed to try hypnotherapy for both her weight problems and her dysphonia. Four weeks later, she had lost a stone and her dysphonia was improving.

There are other problems which may exacerbate a communication disorder. Typical examples are found in clients who have voice disorders and who smoke a lot. Their smoking prevents voice therapy from being of benefit as the vocal cords are in a constant state of irritation because of the smoke. Hypnosis will sometimes help some clients to give up smoking and, if this is achieved, it would enhance the progress made during voice therapy.

## Conclusions

It would seem clear that hypnotherapy is an effective and useful adjunct in the treatment of most communication disorders whether they be psychogenic or organic in etiology. It can not only be used to relax clients but also to give them reassurance and confidence to cope with stressful and communicatively difficult situations. Hypnotherapy is also useful in helping to identify and deal with maintaining and contributing factors which may be perpetuating the communication disorder and which may need to be treated before the core communication problem can be addressed, not necessarily by the speech therapist if these are outside his field of competence. Hypnotherapy may also help clients to learn new behaviours and speech patterns, and overcome maladaptive ones.

# CHAPTER 6
# Use of Hypnosis in Physical and Related Conditions

## Fred Frazer

This chapter will deal with the use of hypnosis as an adjunct to other physical therapies, in the treatment of various neuro-muscular and some of the most frequently met clinical conditions. It is based on the author's practical application of hypnosis within the British National Health Service (NHS) over a period of twenty years.

Most conditions are considered against three main elements; confidence boosting or motivation, pain relief, and training, since all of these are involved, irrespective of the condition, in rehabilitation. In the first place, a patient requiring rehabilitation needs motivation to get better, and irrespective of the patient's age, the therapist needs to find a way of motivating the patient to get better and hypnosis can help to determine this motivating factor.

Pain relief is one area where hypnosis has been used for centuries and its use in the 18th century by such individuals as Elliotson and Esdaile is well documented. More recently workers such as Hilgard and Hilgard (1983), Moon and Moon (1984) and Sacerdote (1982) have each contributed examples of the value of hypnosis in pain relief.

Most patients who require physical therapy will be experiencing pain to some degree. The principles of pain relief will be the same no matter what the nature of the pain is, and can be applied to any patient irrespective of the cause of the pain. A patient who suffers an injury or who has undergone an operation will also, to some degree, lose confidence, not only in himself but also in that part of the body which has been affected. The methods used to relieve this loss of confidence can be applied to any condition and to any patient.

Any rehabilitation of any injury requires systematic training of various muscles and joints. Many of these exercises are unpleasant and painful and require considerable motivation to ensure that the patient complies with the instructions. Compliance by patients with instructions is estimated as no more than 50% (Ley, 1979). The use of hypnosis has been shown to increase compliance (Wagstaff, 1981) and the value of hypnosis in this area cannot be overstated.

While the term trance is used throughout this chapter, the term is in this instance used as a shorthand description of the patient's state as the author has not made any attempt to determine trance depth and indeed makes no attempt to induce trance in the conventional ways of eye fixation as described earlier. Instead, a simple instruction to "close your eyes" followed by instructions to concentrate on the "sound of my voice" is sufficient induction.

## Rehabilitation

There is within rehabilitation a wide range of conditions that can be helped because most of the subjects experience at various stages, pain, loss of function, restriction of movement and loss of confidence. All of these conditions can be positively affected using hypnosis as an adjunct to other more conventional therapies. One of the major problems in any dyadic therapeutic interaction is the difficulty in getting a patient to follow instructions, particularly if the exercises suggested are painful or difficult to perform. Furthermore, there is no way of ensuring that instructions are carried out and relevant research (Rissman, 1987), shows that up to 50% of patients do not comply with treatment instructions. In consequence, it becomes a dual problem of communication and motivation. It is usually accepted that where there is a problem of communication, the problem is likely to lie with the sender rather than the receiver. It is clear that any procedure which will enhance concentration, facilitate communication and increase motivation, such as hypnosis, will be a valuable reinforcement to rehabilitation. It is in this role that hypnosis can be used without risking the charge that it is a panacea for all ills.

### *General Physical Trauma*

The effects of trauma will include pain, swelling, bruising and loss of movement. These effects are associated with most injuries and the principles of treatment apply equally to the other sub-sections outlined above. There are, however, minor differences related to each which will be highlighted below. While it is improbable that a patient with a minor injury will require hypnosis, there will always be a small number who, for various reasons, will exaggerate the effect of the most trivial injury.

It is recognised that circulation can be affected by the use of hypnosis (Meyer, 1989) and this phenomenon is utilised to reduce the swelling and bruising accompanying most injuries. In this way, both swelling and bruising will more rapidly subside, pain will be reduced and rehabilitation accelerated. One routine which can be utilised is given as an example. The patient is put in the hypnotic trance using one of the methods described in Chapter 3. Following a deepening routine the suggestions can commence.

> "Because you are now deeply relaxed, your subconscious mind is totally receptive to any suggestions placed there for your own benefit. Today, I am going to concentrate on your circulation because the blood flowing around your body will help your injury to repair by bringing oxygen and foodstuffs to the damaged cells and by removing carbon dioxide and waste products to take them to be broken down and excreted. All of

this will help your bruising and swelling to be reduced much more quickly. Because the blood vessels, called the 'arterioles', are influenced by your nervous system and because they can be increased in diameter by *forty times, your subconscious mind can help you to increase your circulation which in turn can accelerate the healing of your injury." (*Keele and Neil, 1978)

The therapist can of course vary the message during this part of the procedure, so that it is personalised to the patient being treated. The terms utilised can be modified but it is useful to have a basic framework which can be elaborated upon or can prevent awkward silences while the therapist thinks of something to say.

All of the benefits of increased circulation can then be described before proceeding to the instruction.

"Your sub-conscious mind can boost your circulation anytime you wish, provided you follow the instructions that I give you. Because your subconscious mind never sleeps, it will obey your instructions by day and night, helping your injury to get better quickly.

"As you are lying there, listening to the sound of my voice, you can feel your heart beating more strongly and you can feel the blood surging through your body, in fact your body will begin to feel warm. Indeed, you can make any part of your body feel warm just by concentrating on it."

Let us assume that the subject has an injured left leg.

"Concentrate on your leg. With each breath out, feel your leg getting warmer as the circulation to it increases. Now concentrate on your injury and feel the warmth easing the discomfort. Now I want you to visualise your injury in your mind and I want you to see the circulation opening up around it, dissolving the swelling and carrying it away, making it better."

Allow the subject some moments before continuing.

"In order to maintain this progress, you must practise your self-hypnosis several times each day as each time you do so, you will reinforce the instructions to your subconscious mind."

The patient can then be awakened from his trance and, if necessary, given a customised tape to use at home.

This approach can be used with any injury or condition which will be helped by increasing the circulation and this applies to most patients except for haemophiliacs or those with acute inflammation. The latter will benefit from a circulatory response but this should be preceded by an attempt to influence the body's immune system, and in turn the infection underlying the inflammation.

## Pain relief

Pain is a term used to describe a mental reaction to what is usually a physical trauma. Many words are used to describe pain such as "pinching", "boring", "cramping", "burning", "wrenching", "gripping", and so on. In fact, Melzack and Torgerson (1971) have assembled 102 words used to describe varying degrees of pain. In spite of the diversity of terminology used, these researchers found that substantial numbers of words have the same relative intensity scale for people of widely divergent backgrounds.

In any discussion on pain, two factors must be considered – "pain threshold" and "measuring techniques". Pain threshold is the term used to describe the level of stimulus necessary for pain to be subjectively perceived and is usually regarded as being the minimum stimulus required. For example, a finger placed on the back of the hand will be perceived as pressure which, if the finger is forced down increasingly firmly, will eventually be perceived as pain. The point along the gradient of pressure where pain is initially perceived is described, in this example, as the "pain threshold".

Variations in social, cultural and educational background, as well as differences in personality and individual perceptual processes, also have an influence on the pain threshold. Painful injuries sustained during a rugby match, which at the time are shrugged off, would produce quite different reactions under different circumstances. Similarly, soldiers in the heat of battle may be unaware that they have been injured. The pain threshold is therefore, a widely fluctuating measure which seems to be linked with anxiety. People going into hospital will worry about the possible pain of operation and this worry will in turn lower their pain threshold and sensitise their perception of the actual pain.

Pain therefore, is a phenomenon which nearly everyone has experienced, which few can adequately describe and even fewer, objectively measure. Some attempt must be made to measure pain if pain-relieving treatments are being provided in order to determine their efficacy. Before using case studies to illustrate the use of hypnosis in pain relief, the method of measurement used by the author is described below.

As can be seen in the diagram opposite, this "pain thermometer" provides a visual analogue scale which is easy to read and which includes a condensation of the whole range of subjective expression of pain. The scale has five points with, at either ends, "no pain" and "as much pain as I can bear", being self-explanatory. "Little pain" is a pain which is tolerable. "Quite a lot of pain" describes a level of pain which would require the use of analgesics, while "very bad pain" is a level of pain which will disrupt function and will require specific treatment.

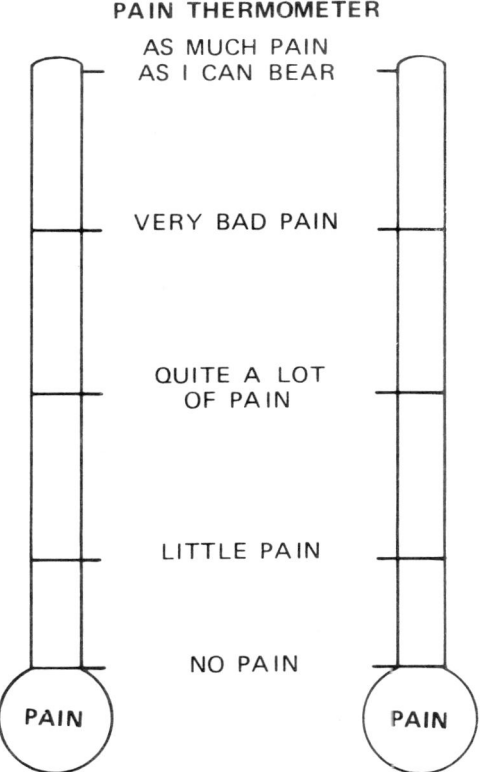

Patients are presented with the pain thermometer before a treatment begins and asked to identify the point on the scale which they feel most accurately represents their pain. This point is marked with the date and the pain thermometer is filed away. A similar procedure is carried out at each subsequent attendance, and upon completion of the course of treatment, the collection of pain thermometer readings are transferred onto a graph. This method of pain measurement has been in use in the South Birmingham Health Authority Physiotherapy Department, in the United Kingdom, for ten years and provides a baseline against which treatment for the relief of pain can be assessed.

It is possible, using hypnosis, to completely eliminate pain in certain subjects. In others, it is possible to change the pain into a different sensation such as warmth, while in most subjects it is possible to reduce the accompanying anxiety, and in consequence, reduce the discomfort to a more tolerable level. As most pain is accompanied by muscular tension or even muscle spasm, the use of hypnosis to break this cycle of 'pain —> tension —> increased pain', is particularly effective because hypnosis can produce relaxation as well as a reduction in anxiety and tension.

## Post Operative Pain
### Case Study 1

Susan was an eighteen year old with a chronic right sciatica of some six months duration, following the removal of a lumbar disc. Her X-rays, which included discograms, were normal and on referral by her surgeon, she was waiting for an appointment at a pain clinic; there was no apparent muscle wasting in either leg.

She had been fine for some months following her operation but the pain had gradually increased and she demonstrated diminished reflexes in the right leg. She described an "aching pain" in her back and a "raging pain" running down the back of her right leg to mid-calf. She was taking eight Fortral daily, was on anti-depressants and used Mogadon to get to sleep, she had spent eleven weeks on total bed-rest and had been very "depressed" the previous fortnight. Following induction which was rapid, a relaxation and confidence-building routine was carried out, and following deepening, she was asked to practise visualising her pain as a shape or a substance which she could identify in her mind.

A tape was prepared and her second treatment was used to help her develop her image of her pain as an entity. Several methods were used to try and attack the pain, including visualising her "shape" being slowly shrouded in cloud, being slowly immersed in oil, and so on. This routine did allow her to control her pain but it usually returned shortly after her treatment.

During the following day she suddenly awoke after listening to her tape with "a horrible feeling of fear" and began crying. Since that episode, she had been unable to relax and felt that she had lost her confidence. Following reassurance, she was put into her trance using the neck touch method described below, and the following routine was used after a prolonged deepening period.

> "Today we are going to work together to eliminate your pain completely. As you know, you are feeling very tense and upset and this will make your pain seem much worse. As you begin to relax, you will find your pain becoming more bearable and with this awareness you will develop much more confidence.
>
> "I am now going to take you down deeper than you have ever been before. I am going to hold your hand so that you know that you are quite safe and won't be worried by the strange sensation that you are going to experience."

The subject's right hand was then placed in the palm of the author's right hand with the instruction:

> "If you feel anxious at any time, just hold on tightly to my hand.
> "You are now going to feel that you are sinking down into total relaxation, total blackness. With every breath out, you will feel yourself sinking down - and down - deeper - and deeper."

These last few instructions are given to coincide with the subject's breathing.

"You are now totally relaxed, more relaxed than you have ever been before. We are going to remove your pain completely.

"I am now going to place my hand on the painful part of your leg. I want you to concentrate on where my hand is touching you and as you do so, you will find your leg beginning to get very warm in this part. Concentrate hard ...... feel your leg becoming warmer ...... your leg is getting very warm where I am touching it."

These instructions were repeated several times and it was interesting to note that the subject's leg was wet with perspiration at this point.

"The sensation of heat that you feel will remain after you waken, you will feel pleasantly warm and the warmth will remove your pain. From now on, whenever you feel pain you will be able to remove it provided you practise your relaxation and follow my instructions on your tape."

Susan's tape was modified to include the above routine and she was asked to use it daily.

By the end of the following week, Susan was totally pain-free and within a fortnight had begun a two month holiday job as an evening waitress in a busy restaurant. Some five years later, during the preparation of this chapter, the author was asked to see this patient again as she had been involved in an RTA in the USA and had suffered a crush fracture of her 8th dorsal vertebra, and was in considerable pain. On this occasion, hypnosis was extremely effective in both producing pain relief and, more importantly, in the boosting of her confidence and motivation. A tape was prepared which she used for the first two weeks and which was then updated when her back support was fitted. This technique of pain removal can be very effective in certain individuals. It simply involves the replacement of pain by another, less unpleasant sensation, in this case heat. Other subjects may respond to cold or to suggestions of numbness.

Another method which can be utilised is the imposition of "glove" anaesthesia where the subject receives a suggestion while under hypnosis that on awakening his hand will be quite numb and devoid of any feeling. The subject is then awakened and the success of the anaesthesia is tested. If the subject has proved receptive, the trance is reintroduced and the anaesthesia in the hand is then transferred by suggestion to whatever part of the body it is desired. This method is highly effective in about 20% of subjects.

## *Cancer Pain*

*Case Study 2*

The author was called to the orthopaedic ward to see Bill, a fit-looking 52 year old man with cancer, who had secondary tumours in his left upper arm, his pelvis, right thigh and two of his lumbar vertebrae. One vertebra had collapsed and he was suffering constant sciatic pain. He was on Bromptons cocktail, Diamorphine and Cocaine in a sweetened alcohol base per res natura (whenever required) and the surgeon was concerned at the quantity of this drug required to allow him to rest. Any attempts at moving him resulted in strong protests from Bill, who could not tolerate the pain involved. On entry to the ward, a commotion was heard. It was Bill shouting and writhing about on his bed. He appeared to be in intense pain.

It was quite clear that any attempt at hypnosis with the subject in this condition would be doomed to failure and it was arranged with the staff and Bill that hypnosis would begin as soon as his drugs had settled him down. On the second visit thirty minutes later, Bill was quite calm and induction was carried out.

It is generally believed that hypnotic induction is best performed in a quiet, relaxed atmosphere but this seems to be more important to the therapist rather than to the subject. If the former is confident, then it will not matter where or when he is asked to induce a hypnotic trance.

In Bill's case, he was in the middle bed of a six bed bay in a modern ward. His bay was opposite the sluice and the constant noise of a busy hospital ward formed a background to the induction process. This noise, of course, was not a distraction to Bill as he had been living with it for several weeks and was quite used to it. It was however, a distraction to the hypnotherapist.

Because of the seriousness of Bill's condition, it was decided to attempt to anaesthetise his painful leg in order that he could have his dangerously high levels of powerful drugs reduced, and to assist him to regain some normal function. Experience has shown that the production of anaesthesia is facilitated by the subject's expectation of success, by the reputation of the hypnotist and by the confidence which he displays.

All of these factors were present on this occasion. Following induction, Bill's trance was deepened and the following routine was carried out:

> "Now that you are deeply relaxed, I want you to concentrate on your right leg. As you concentrate you will be conscious of its weight resting on the bed. It will soon begin to feel heavier - so heavy that it feels as if it is sinking into the bed. Concentrate hard."

This set of instructions was repeated slowly and followed with:

> "As your leg feels heavier, it will begin to become quite numb. All feeling will disappear completely (pause). Your leg is now beginning to lose all sensation; soon it will feel quite numb."

Some time was spent in reinforcing this suggestion and finally, Bill was told his leg was totally numb and that he would not be able to feel it being touched. At this point, the author pushed a hypodermic needle through the calf of his right leg and left it in situ. Bill was wakened after being told that his leg would feel totally numb when he woke up but that he would be able to use it quite normally.

On awakening, he displayed astonishment that his leg was quite pain-free. This astonishment was compounded when the needle was pointed out to him. This is a test for anaesthesia which the author often carries out using a sterile needle and a steri swab to prepare the skin surface.

Bill was seen on the ward twice daily for two days and had ceased to require any drugs other than one panadol each bedtime. He was walking the length of the ward with assistance from the physiotherapy staff. On the third day, his wife was taught the induction process, given a tape and a set of written instructions. Bill was given a post-hypnotic suggestion that he would be able to comply with his wife's instructions and he was discharged home on the fifth day, pain-free, off drugs and happy to be going home, where he remained until he died three months later.

In cases such as Bill's, it is worth trying an all or nothing approach, but it must be remembered that pain, although unpleasant, is a symptom, and that straightforward symptom removal is fraught with hazard and should not be carried out except in extreme cases such as Bill's. It is inadvisable therefore, to remove pain totally except in cases such as that described above, because pain is a symptom of a pathological condition. If the source of the pain was, for example, a pathological fracture or an abscess of some kind or a tumour, and the pain were removed, the patient would be unable to report any other symptoms until, perhaps, the condition had become extremely serious. It is most important that any attempt to relieve pain is with the full agreement of the patient's doctor and with the hypnotherapist's full knowledge of the actual underlying condition.

## Post Traumatic Pain

### Case Study 3

Joan was a fourteen year old girl who had been in a car crash and had suffered a whiplash injury to her neck, which eventually developed into a spasmodic torticollis, resulting in her missing three months' school. She was being taught at home by a peripatetic teacher as she was preparing for her 'O' levels.

She was a good subject and under hypnosis her neck movements were full. Following a post-hypnotic suggestion that on awakening she would be pain-free and her head would be held straight, she was awakened and was able to move her head around normally. During a four week period, she continued to improve, but with the occasional lapse into spasm, and returned to full-time school at the end of this period.

This condition is very difficult to cure unless, as in this case, there is a clear case of physical injury preceding the torticollis. Joan was being considered for surgery by the neuro-surgeons, but this was no longer necessary thanks to a combination of hypnosis and enthusiastic physiotherapy .

Hypnosis can be used in any condition where pain, immobility and loss of motivation can all contribute to an overall demoralisation of the sufferer, with consequent problems for recovery. The above features most commonly accompany rheumatoid arthritis as an ongoing burden for the sufferer and hypnosis is valuable with these patients in two main ways; the promotion of relaxation and the enhancement of motivation to encourage the patient to continue the struggle against this crippling condition.

## Confidence

While the consideration of confidence may belong more properly within a chapter on psychosomatic conditions, it is nevertheless mentioned here as there are many patients, whose loss of confidence, following either illness or injury is often as disabling as the surgical condition.

The above cases demonstrate that hypnosis can be a successful analgesic. It is unclear whether such an effect is due to some physiological process or whether it is simply a result of suggestion which depends for its success upon the relationship between hypnotist and patient.

There is a growing number of systems and books about systems, designed to boost self-confidence. The proliferation of these may reflect the growing pressures of life in today's society. They also reflect the extent of the problem and there can be few readers who have not at some time experienced a loss of confidence.

The bulk of the advertising industry is targeted on individual's need to boost his confidence. People worry about their height, shape, weight, intelligence, clothes, smell and so on. For every worry, an entrepreneur somewhere has developed a product which his advertisers assure us will conceal our imperfections and boost our confidence. There is a clear link between confidence and self-esteem and it is rare for a person who does not feel good about himself to feel confident.

The following case history illustrates one of the common causes of loss of confidence and helps to show how the problem can be helped by hypnosis.

*Case Study 4*

George was a 56 year old consultant surgeon who had undergone surgery for cancer of his colon. Prior to that, he had been ill for six months with a gastric ulcer. He was now free of malignancy and physically back to normal, but he felt depressed and totally lacking in confidence. On the day he saw me, he had been unable to complete an operation, bursting into tears during the final stages, and had to hand over to his registrar. He said that recently he often cried for no reason, he felt more nervous than usual, and during his out-patient clinics, he felt depressed between patients. He went to bed at 10 o'clock and woke at 5.00 am each morning, yet he felt tired all of the time. He was eating normally and "had no problems with his work." His spare time was spent watching television and he "just couldn't be bothered" with his hobbies.

George was provided with his individual tape which contained the material already described, and was given three treatments in a two week period. By this time he felt better, although he still had one or two bad days. He told the author that his ten year old son had taken control of him and used to make him lie down on the bed and listen to his tape; in fact, they used to listen to it together. He resumed his normal surgical case load without any further problems and five years later is still working as a full-time consultant surgeon in the National Health Service in the United Kingdon, a fact which I was able to confirm at the time of writing this chapter.

Irrespective of the reason for loss of confidence, the treatment is broadly similar and will include the provision of a tape, which is used during auto-hypnosis sessions by the subject. With this method, subjects can then tailor their treatment to suit their particular case. There is a very thin dividing line between being and not being confident, and the operator must remember to promote positive images, particularly during the early stages of treatment. Loss of confidence can, in most cases, be successfully reversed using hypnosis and is one other example where hypnosis is vastly superior to drugs.

## Sports and training

### Physical Training

The problems associated with training can be either physical or psychological. Both can be present together, or be related to one another. A nagging pain following a training workout will probably create anxiety in a sportsman, which in turn will be reflected in diminished performance, and possibly neurosis or depression. Many athletes are extremely sensitive to their own physical and mental states and even minor changes can produce reactions quite out of proportion to the cause. Many such individuals therefore, may be described as neurotic or obsessional.

Although hypnosis is being suggested as possibly useful in sport, it is clear that there is also a significant role within general rehabilitation. Some people may overcome physical inadequacies by a combination of persistence and determination, and a strong will to win, while others with the physical attributes and skills, fail because they lack the psychological qualities. The latter point is clearly demonstrated in the case of several well-known boxers who, although perfect physical specimens and always fully prepared for each fight, fail to win against opponents because of an inability to sustain, or to capitalise on, an attack. Although they have the skill and the strength, and are adequately physically prepared, psychologically, they are ill-equipped to win.

### Road Running

Although this is essential in order to build up basic stamina, and is probably one of the most boring training methods available, there are a number of top athletes who run enormous distances each week. They will confirm that great determination and persistence is required in order to force themselves out onto a training run, despite aching joints and tired muscles. Once the body is warmed up however, the running becomes pleasant and the runner achieves a "high" caused by the release of endorphins thought to be triggered off by the running itself. This "high" is manifested in a feeling of well-being, a feeling of being confident and in control, and must be familiar to many athletes, even to the overweight, "plodding round the block" jogger.

Auto-hypnosis is valuable in running of this kind as it can be used during the lengthy periods of time involved, in several ways. Visualisation of the body as a machine, with concentration on one particular system at a time, will help distract runners from their fatigue. Alternatively, they can picture their participation in some future event and rehearse all aspects of it, defined as ideo-motor training. This involves athletes visualising themselves performing the various stages of an event. For example, they can mentally play a tennis match and visualise their service, and so on.

The visualisation of different body systems can also be used in conjunction with biofeedback methods designed to increase, for example, blood-flow to the muscles, or to raise the heart-beat just before a race starts. This can also be practised during the running period. Several other self-regulating schemes can be utilised during the long, time-consuming training runs. These are designed either to reduce stress and competition anxiety, or conversely to "psyche up" the athlete to an optimal state prior to an event.

A training run can be used in several ways, both for the direct physical effect produced and for the psychological preparation that can be carried out during the time involved, thus doubling its value and greatly reducing the inevitable boredom attached to long distance running.

## *Weight Training*

Most rehabilitation will include some form of weight training in their training schedules. Apart from building additional muscular strength, weight training is valuable because subjects can, with careful management, graduate their training and maintain a peak level of performance without becoming stale. Staleness is simply an inability to perform at a customary level and may result from over-training or from too long a period spent in maintaining an optimum level of performance. Because weight training is repetitive and athletes are working against a dead weight, their mental attitude is important and auto-hypnosis can be used either to trigger off the aggression required to lift a heavy weight or alternatively, to increase the efficacy of the rest period between sets of repetitions.

## *Specialised Exercises*

These will depend upon the condition involved, although most will be designed to help various parts of the body to stretch to a maximum without injury.

## *Sport*

Rigorous physical training, skill, talent and enthusiasm, coupled with strong motivation to succeed, will often ensure success in sport. Even those with little natural talent can, with hard work and practice, develop their sporting skills to an acceptable level.

Any athletes who have utilised the above techniques, whether they are merely "leisure" athletes or international sportsmen, have reported positive results.

## *Case Study 5*

Andrew was a 24 year old trainee chartered accountant who at the time he attended for treatment, was studying for his final exams. He was a cross-country runner who had been in a car crash and had suffered a transverse fracture of his left patella which had been pinned. Six months later, he had approximately 1 1/2" of muscle wasting in his left quadriceps and complained that he was unable to train because his knee kept letting him down. His knee flexion was slightly limited and he had no pain or swelling. His main complaint was a fear of falling over and a feeling that he was "unbalanced and totally wrong."

Apart from the muscle wasting and the limitation of knee flexion to about 80° of normal, there was nothing else physically wrong and he had been referred for hypnosis in an attempt to remove his mental block against fully exercising his knee. He said he felt his determination had been lost; "I feel a defeatist attitude." He was also worried about his forthcoming exams and this, plus his problem with his knee, appeared to combine to keep him in a cycle of despair.

He was given the standard treatment which included induction, relaxation and deepening routines, and given the instruction that he would begin training again from that evening. He was also given instructions related to his study. On his first week, he managed to run four miles and to do half an hour of exercises each day. His knee had not swollen but he reported having to stop from time to time because he felt that he was going to fall over.

On the third week, he was running two miles each evening and had graduated to straight leg raising with a twenty pound weight. He had tripped and fallen during a run, injuring his knee which swelled slightly, but this had subsided. By the end of two months, he was including step-ups and squats in his training routine, playing squash twice weekly and doing training runs three times a week. His muscle bulk had increased by 1/2" and he felt quite confident about his knee. He was discharged having had a course of six treatments spread over an eight week period.

Another area which embodies many of the features described above is that of fractures, which share many similarities with sports injuries, particularly those of the femur and tibia which can have a lengthy healing period. Hypnosis is useful at all stages of rehabilitation, during the fixation stage hypnosis can help to promote healing by increasing the circulation within the area and by enhancing the motivation of the subject to ensure that exercises are practised regularly. When the plaster of Paris is removed, hypnosis will assist in the mobilising stage of the rehabilitation.

## General medical procedures

One final area where hypnosis is of very considerable value, even though it is not exactly considered to be part of rehabilitation, is the use of hypnosis in investigative or, indeed, certain clinical treatments. For example, cystoscopys, colposcopys, proctoscopys, endoscopys and of course, the insertion of drips, chest drains, or anything to do with dressing of wounds.

One case study very clearly demonstrates the value of hypnosis and this concerns a little boy aged nine who had been born with very serious heart defects and had been on the Harefield Hospital waiting list for three years for a heart transplant. During that time, he was in such poor condition that he had to attend the Children's Hospital every month, and sometimes more frequently, to have his thorax drained of excess fluid because he was suffering from cardiac failure. He also needed a drip to be inserted which very often required a cut down because of the collapse of his peripheral circulation. In consequence, when the child was going into hospital, he had to be held down by nurses while the doctor tried to insert the chest drains or the drips, and this was very traumatic for the child and, indeed, for the parents. The author was telephoned at midnight, one night after one of these episodes, by a consultant anaesthetist who asked "could hypnosis help this child?" The child was seen the following day and was put into a light trance and, over a period of some weeks, he became accustomed to holding hypodermic needles in his hand and eventually got to the stage where he was able to put himself into hypnosis. From that stage onwards, he was able to go into hospital and receive all of the above procedures without a murmur: the difference which was made to his day to day existence was highly significant.

It is therefore, doubly important that anyone connected with health care, of whatever kind, needs to consider hypnosis as a useful addition to their clinical skills because if it even helps one patient out of a hundred, especially a patient such as little Johnny, it is well worth trying, and not least because it is free, it does not do the patient any harm, there are no side effects, and it can prove extremely effective.

## Skin problems

### *Burns*

Burns patients derive benefit from hypnosis, particularly during the extremely painful removal and application of wound dressings. Research has demonstrated (Moore, 1983; May, 1983) that hypnosis can help to accelerate healing and can be particularly valuable in the case of burns rehabilitation.

### *Associated Conditions*

Patients with skin conditions can derive significant relief from hypnosis, particularly those patients whose condition is exacerbated by scratching, as a post hypnotic suggestion to re-direct this action can be remarkably effective. It is well recognised that very few patients with a skin condition are, what is described as "ill", although they use various drugs and ointments to ease irritation and reduce discomfort. Many suffer significant psychological distress associated with the skin problem and in such patients it is well worth trying hypnosis as a form of therapy.

### Case Study 6

John, referred by a dermatologist, suffered from psoriasis psittica for as long as he could remember which got worse at times of stress. He was a 20 year old university student in the middle of his end of year exams and had just finished a four year relationship with a girlfriend so it was hardly surprising to find on his first visit that he was stressed, lacking in confidence and almost covered in psoriatic eruptions. His hands were bandaged as he had scratched them until they had bled and become infected. His tar-based ointment and steroid treatment was not helping and he viewed hypnosis as a desperate last resort.

Following routine induction, ego-strengthening techniques were utilised, a tape was prepared and he was given an additional instruction, which can be used for all patients where scratching is a problem.

> "Today you are going to do two things when you leave me; the first is you will obtain a piece of leather and have it stitched to your trouser waist or a pocket. Then at any time you feel the urge to scratch, your fingers will immediately seek out this piece of leather, and when you scratch it, all itchiness will disappear. Secondly, any time your fingers stray to any other part of your body (named if required) your subconscious mind will immediately make you aware of what you are doing and you will consciously stop."

Added to these specific instructions, it is useful to suggest that each time the subject practises auto-hypnosis, using his tape, the circulation to his skin will increase and the skin will feel warm and the irritation will subside.

This approach can be used for any skin condition to promote healing, to reduce irritation and to prevent scratching; it has proved successful with many patients.

A particularly interesting use of hypnosis is illustrated by the following case history where hypnosis enabled a boy of thirteen to accept his contact lenses.

*Case Study 7*

While this case study concerns irritation of eyes, it nevertheless shows many similarities, in terms of symptoms, with skin complaints.

Adrian, a serious, studious boy, had been prescribed "hard" contact lenses to help correct deteriorating vision. He did not mind wearing glasses but he did not like putting the contact lenses in his eyes and in fact had developed a block against even attempting to insert the lenses, particularly the left eye.

He was given a routine induction, ego boost and the following instruction.

> "You will treat the next few weeks as an experiment which you will record as follows; the date, what you did, how you felt, note the period of discomfort and how long you kept the lenses in, and finally how you felt when you removed them."

Adrian complied and on his return the following week had faithfully recorded:

He managed to get both lenses in over a period of 3 minutes and observed that the discomfort lessened over a period. However, he had been successful on only two out of the seven days.

He was given a tape which repeated the above instructions as well as reassuring him that "it was no big deal" if he had some periods of failure.

Following a further three visits Adrian has had no more problems and now wears his lenses every day at school, his mother's comment sums up this case study: "A success story you might say!"

## Conclusions

This chapter provides a small number of examples where hypnosis has been used with patients who have undergone rehabilitation. There is little doubt that most patients who are recovering from either illness or injury will benefit to some degree by the use of hypnosis as an adjunct to their physical therapy and, because of its ease of application and significant lack of any side effects, it should always be considered as a part of the rehabilitation process.

# CHAPTER 7
# Miscellaneous Conditions

## S. Abudarham

This chapter has been included in this book in recognition of some of the conditions met by members of the health care team which often present with and are related to the core problem. A typical example of this has already been mentioned in Chapter 5 and is illustrated by the case of the 'functional' dysphonic lady whose overweight caused her to have a low self-esteem and both of these problems were clearly related to her dysphonia.

It is always important when dealing with clients with these conditions to check if they are under medical supervision, medication, etc. With the client's prior agreement, his doctor should be contacted in writing and asked if he has any objection to hypnotherapy for his client and his condition. A letter should also include a question such as "in your opinion, is there any reason, medical or otherwise, contra-indicating hypnotherapy." Self-referring clients should be asked if they have sought medical help for their problem and if not, why not. The answer is often revealing and could reflect factors contributing to the core problem. These may need to be addressed or may in themselves be contra-indicative to hypnotherapy. On occasions, self referring clients may not wish their doctors to be contacted, sometimes because their doctor has refused to recommend hypnotherapy for good reason or because of prejudice against this mode of therapy, or because the client is scared that such a request might be turned down, or is worried that the doctor might get offended that he is being 'told' what to do or that someone else's opinion/therapy is being sought. In cases such as smokers, this is unlikely to be an important issue and by and large it is probably quite safe to treat clients to help them reduce smoking through hypnotherapy, without a medical opinion. However, even in these cases, it may still be advisable to ask clients if they suffer from, or have been or are being treated for, a medical (or psychiatric) condition. Where prior medical clearance may well be very important, is in the case of clients wishing to reduce weight. A typical example is the diabetic client who wishes to reduce weight. If the hypnotherapist is not aware of his diabetes and recommends a 'popular' diet comprising a reduction of carbohydrates, this could be fatal for the diabetic client who may need a certain amount of carbohydrates. More often than not, this type of client is aware of this.

### Smoking

This 'habit' is not as easy to get rid of through hypnosis as many people often claim. Some cases I have treated enjoyed temporary success from a single session of hypnosis. The fact that they have then requested further hypnotherapy from me indicated how vulnerable they still were to a relapse. I have however, met a small number of ex-smokers who several years later had not smoked at all even though they had only received one hypnosis session.

However, because smoking is addictive, smokers are usually very dependent on the 'drug' and it takes time before the body can get used to being without the nicotine. Hypnosis on its own is very often not enough and the client's full commitment has to be established and secured. In Chapter 2, I referred to a client whose motivation had been prompted by his mother's death from lung cancer the previous day; a powerful motivator indeed which nevertheless turned out to be ephemeral. Generally, and before taking on a smoker, I advise the client that a minimum number of sessions is likely to be required and possibly some follow-ups. If the client is not agreeable to this plan, I rarely take them on for treatment. If on the other hand he is agreeable, I offer him an appointment for an initial and lengthy session of between one hour and an hour and a half. During the interview, I obtain information in particular about the number and brand of cigarettes he smokes and also the brand he hates most. Other aspects of his habit such as how long he has been smoking, at what times during the day and before and after which particular events/activities he tends to smoke. Very often smoking, eating and/or drinking have become a mutually inclusive chain of events so that a smoker will light up a cigarette immediately he has poured himself a drink, or after he has finished a meal. He might do the same before opening his post or answering the telephone. Are there any particular affective states in which he tends to smoke most frequently. Information about his marital status, size of family, etc., may be useful and may be incorporated during therapy. In order to establish how dependent he is on cigarettes, I may ask what he would do if he found himself without cigarettes. Questions about his health may also be appropriate in particular with regards to whether he is overweight, suffers from any vascular conditions or any smoking-related medical condition. All this information may prove its usefulness subsequently and be incorporated during hypnotherapy.

If it is decided that hypnotherapy may be helpful, the client is told that he can not and must not depend on the therapist waving a magic wand and that without much effort on the client's part, his urge to smoke will disappear. A date three or four weeks hence is agreed upon, on which the client will totally give up smoking. If the client insists that he wishes to give up that same day, I usually explain that this is usually not as effective as 'weaning' himself away from the habit over a longer period of time but having given him this advice, if he is not agreeable, his suggestion must be considered in a rational way and he is advised on the need for a follow up session two weeks or a month later to monitor his progress. This can be achieved as well by asking the client to keep telephone contact on agreed times and dates as appropriate.

There are then several approaches that can be taken. The one I prefer aims to help the client to break the link between smoking and, food and drink.

Under hypnosis, he is thus instructed that he can smoke any time he wishes during the day or night except during half an hour before and after breakfast, lunch or supper, and half an hour before he goes to bed. Before he retires, he should brush his teeth to try and eliminate the taste of nicotine from his mouth. In the morning he should do likewise and in addition drink some fruit juice. Following breakfast and all subsequent meals, he must not smoke for at least half an hour. He must maintain this regime for one whole week and report on his progress, feelings etc. at the next session. The first session finishes with an appropriate ego-strengthening routine and, after termination, discussion and reiteration of the suggestions made under hypnosis. During the ego strengthening, the information obtained during the interview can usually be employed but always in a positive manner. The client should be encouraged to think of the health and financial benefits of not smoking, how much personal hygiene will improve and how more socially acceptable his new behaviour will become.

A similar routine is followed during subsequent sessions except that on the second, the client is instructed to extend pre- and post meals periods of non-smoking to one hour. On the third session, the 'no-smoking' time is increased to one and a half hours and in addition he is told he can only smoke the brand of cigarettes he had previously declared he likes least.

I introduce this strategy the week before the client is due to give up smoking because it does not usually take a client long to acquire a taste for even his most hated brand of cigarette if it is the only one available to him. In one case, a female client had said that one thing she would never smoke was cigars. During the course of treatment, and at the appropriate point, I suggested she should smoke only slim panatella cigars, from then on till we next met. After recoiling at the suggestion, she agreed to do this. At the next session, she reported she had hated smoking the cigars during the first few days but that after the fourth day or so, she had started acquiring a taste for them and was even inhaling the smoke to maximise satisfaction. She thought that given a week or so she would be smoking as many cigars as she previously had cigarettes.

This programme has several benefits. In the first instance, and as mentioned earlier, it aims to break the link between smoking and food/drink or any other variable associated with the need to smoke. By restricting smoking time rather than asking the client to radically cut it out immediately and altogether, it allows the client a period of time for 'psychological' and 'physiological climb down' during which time he does not need to 'panic' that he is going to give up immediately and without 'a final smoke'. He is also given an opportunity to prepare himself psychologically for the targeted 'quitting day' and experience progressively extended periods of nicotine-free time. For those clients who manage successfully, this experience is often reassuring that they will in fact be able to cope when they finally give up. For those who find this period hard but keep to the agreement, it is nevertheless a good preparatory strategy; in any case these clients are unlikely to succeed if told to give up immediately after the first session. Finally, if the client keeps to the contract, he usually reports that he has smoked less cigarettes than usual. There are of course some exceptions and a few clients have reported that they felt compelled to make up for cigarettes not smoked and those he was about not to smoke during the prescribed abstention periods in the course of the day; however, this has been, in my experience, the exception and not the rule.

It must be reiterated that this programme may not be suitable for all clients. Clients have to be given a lot of support and reassurance, particularly during ego-strengthening routines and continuous reinforcement of the advantages of giving up. They should also be congratulated for their progress so far and reassured that they will be able to cope without any cigarettes when 'quitting day' arrives and after. Some clients complain that they experience withdrawal symptoms, become more irritable, or feel compelled to smoke after going out for dinner with smoking friends who light up after each course. Interestingly, one particular client said that the advantage of giving up smoking with hypnotherapy was that, unlike with other methods, he did not suffer withdrawal symptoms. Others will complain that they are eating more and/or putting on weight. These issues must be discussed seriously and such clients must be helped to develop strategies to deal with these 'obstacles'. If necessary, they need to be incorporated during hypnotherapy. It is often the case that these complaints augur badly and may reflect a weakening of resolve and commitment. This possibility must be raised openly and the client faced with it. In several cases, the problems have been very real and one needs to recognise these, and if necessary help the client resolve them.

*Case Study 1*

Debbie was a very attractive, married 28 year old who was very proud of her very slim figure. During the course of treatment she complained that she was more quickly irritated by her two children than she ever had been before. Strategies for avoiding irritating situations and dealing with those that did occur were discussed; of course, these had to relate to her own circumstances. She was assured that it was not uncommon to feel like this and was encouraged to stick it out as her irritability would reduce as she got more used to not smoking. This approach was reasonably successful. However, a follow up discussion after therapy had been completed and after she had not smoked for a month, revealed that she could not cope with putting on weight, however little, and this was a worse curse than smoking. She reported though, that she had stopped smoking cigarettes and was smoking little cigarillos which were less damaging to her health. Debbie had in fact always been weight-conscious because her mother used to over feed her when she was a child and she had to bear the brunt of cruel teasing from peers.

In fact, many ex-smokers do put on weight and this is not always due to eating more. Nicotine is known to accelerate the digestive process; without it, digestion takes longer and this can result in weight gain. Those who do find that they eat more, can be advised on eating low calorie foods such as carrots, celery, etc., or on drinking low calorie beverages which will satiate their hunger and thirst.

In cases where clients complain that they are not coping, or strongly feel they will not be able to give up completely, despite discussion and three or four hypnotherapy sessions, two possible courses of action can be taken. The first is termination of treatment and acknowledging that hypnotherapy has not worked. The second is to ask the client under hypnosis whether he really wants to give up and if so whether he is ready to do so before termination of treatment. If the answer to the former is positive and to the latter negative, he can be asked to propose a date when he will be more ready to give up. On occasions, clients know that at some point during, or soon after a course of hypnotherapy, they have to tackle a very crucial situation and they get anxious that they will not be able to handle it successfully without the calming effects of smoking. Their anxiety is therefore, so great that no amount of hypnotherapy or ego strengthening will help. In cases when clients seem to lack commitment or will power, they should be asked if there are any imminent events in their life which could be weakening their resolve to give up smoking. When this happens, it is usually advisable to postpone further treatment until such events are over. This type of client is often faced with many such events in his life which may thus make any treatment ineffective and this possibility must be pointed out to him. Hypnotherapy and other techniques such as assertive therapy, relaxation therapy etc., can of course be used to help the client to deal with life's pressures in a more relaxed and confident way and this can be offered to the client.

In my experience prolonged hypnotherapy beyond a maximum of six 'pre-quitting' sessions (four on average) rarely serves any useful purpose and it is much better to postpone treatment and renew the contact at a more favourable time.

On the last session, 'quitting day' should be discussed whilst out of and in hypnosis. It is probably better if that day starts the morning after the last session as the effects of post hypnotic suggestion and ego strengthening are likely to still be strong enough. It is my practice to tell clients that I shall be phoning them the evening before to wish them good luck and offer them a final word of encouragement and reassurance. It is interesting to note how many clients have welcomed such a phone call. One in particular told me I had just caught her on the point of lighting up. My call had made her reconsider and she threw the remaining cigarettes into the dustbin.

Experience has shown that the next two or three months after 'quitting day' are crucial and clients who resume smoking do so during this time. It is for this reason that monitoring their progress is important. This can be done by keeping telephone contact once a week for two or three months so that at appointed dates and times the therapist phones the client to discuss progress, and any problems which the client may be experiencing, or the client agrees to phone the therapist. The latter strategy, I am afraid, is not as reliable as the first. If during such discussions, the therapist feels that the client might benefit from a 'booster' session, this should be offered to the client. In any case, I always recommend such a session at four week intervals following 'quitting day' for three months. It must be said that giving up smoking is not the easiest of tasks. It generally takes more than hypnotherapy on its own and many clients who expected the therapist to wave his 'magic wand' and cure them through the power of 'strong, irresistible , hypnotic suggestion' have been disappointed. Clients must therefore, be told quite plainly that they must also play a positive and active role in their therapy. I sometimes wonder whether many of the 'failures' might be partly due to the absence of post-treatment monitoring and review sessions.

As an ex-smoker myself, and having kept contact with many clients, I reckon that it takes about two years before the yearning for nicotine disappears and even then, it rarely does so completely. Even after 14 years of not smoking cigarettes, on occasions, I feel like a smoke especially after a good meal. I usually advise clients that they may feel like this and that if they can control this urge for a quarter of an hour or so, they will find that the yearning disappears soon after, but those post-prandial 20 minutes may be crucial.

## Weight loss

In this section, I shall not be referring to weight problems due to some pathological eating disorder. Millions of people without any serious psychological or medical problems are forever starting (and giving up) diets simply to reduce their weight. The reasons for this often reflect well publicised medical opinion about the dangers of overweight. Other reasons may include the reduction of physical discomfort attributed to overweight, such as muscular aches and pains, breathlessness at the slightest physical task, or a wish to improve one's appearance and self esteem. Very often, a loss of weight helps the client to improve his social confidence and skills. Many people eat more in response to stress (See Case Study 3 in Chapter 3).

The client referred to a member of a health care profession, other than to a dietician, is not likely to be referred because of a weight problem. However, a weight problem may be part and parcel of the core problem for which the client has been referred, such as illustrated in Case Study 3, in Chapter 5. Another example could be clients referred to physiotherapists, osteopaths, etc. for back pain or any other condition which is directly exacerbated by overweight or obesity. In all cases, one needs to establish how long the problem has persisted, whether any life experiences have brought it about, why the client wishes to reduce weight, what is the cause of the overweight and whether the client is under medical supervision for any dietary problem, or whether he suffers from any condition where the nature of the diet may be important, e.g. diabetes. If this is the case, then a medical opinion and approval for hypnotherapy needs to be sought. Similarly, a client may be suffering from some psychiatric condition which may need professional attention. By and large, I have found that doctors and psychiatrists are often only too happy, if they trust the 'health care' hypnotherapist, to approve of a course of hypnotherapy. If a client is under medical supervision or has got a medical condition, a non-medically qualified hypnotherapist should only agree to use hypnotherapy in consultation with an appropriately qualified person such as a doctor, psychiatrist or dietician. These occasions sometimes arise in the health service when the appropriately qualified person has not got the time or expertise to treat the client with hypnotherapy. Such team work is to be commended. Hypnotherapy in these cases is best used as an adjunct to other therapies. For example, if a client finds it difficult to keep to a recommended diet prescribed by a physician or dietician, hypnotherapy may be able to help him do so.

In cases when a medical condition does not underlie a weight problem, or when no such conditions are associated with it, the treatment is more straight forward and hypnotherapy can be very helpful. Having taken a detailed case history, particularly in relation to the client's eating habits and diet, reasons for wishing to reduce weight, how much weight he wishes to lose, and whether there are situations or times when he tends to overeat, the client is asked how he has tried to control his weight in the past. Sometimes, clients have gone on popular diets acquired from books. If they have been successful previously with a particular diet and they have felt comfortable with it, there is a greater chance that they will want to go on that particular diet again and they may need hypnotherapy to help them develop self discipline and commitment. It is often revealing to ask the client why he has regained weight or why he thinks a diet regime may have failed. The answers have to be taken into consideration when deciding on a treatment plan, and whether a diet is going to be recommended and if so which type.

The most common ways to reduce weight is to either reduce one's food consumption, avoid fattening foods, or a combination of both. Popular diet books will invoke the advantages of a particular diet. Some will argue against the need for weighing every morsel to be eaten, others are restricted to one form of food, e.g. a fruit diet, and even those which claim to be 'medically balanced' can not always agree on what constitutes 'medical balance' in a diet. Variations thus exist and to my mind, the last word on choice of diet is the client's (provided of course there are no medical contraindications). However, a hypnotherapist who has seen many clients for overweight may be able to recommend a particular tried and tested 'popular' diet. One of my preferences is "The Complete Scarsdale Medical Diet" developed by Tarnower and Sinclair Baker (1978). The attraction of the diet is that one does not have to worry about tediously weighing anything, it "averages 1,000 calories or less per day, averages 43 per cent protein, 22.5 per cent fat and 34.5 per cent carbohydrates". The main part of the diet only lasts two weeks and this limit is mandatory. This is followed by a two week "Keep Trim Diet", thus allowing the client to anticipate a reasonably early end to the diet. The menus recommended are not much different to what one might expect in a normal diet (with the omission of alcohol and fatty foods, though limited quantities of protein bread are allowed) and contain variety and much more imagination than many other diets. All these points are very important as they often form the very reasons why clients do not keep to diets. My clients have lost between half and one stone in the two weeks. Weight loss characteristically is greater in the first and second week but some clients have lost between two and four pounds a week on the "Keep Trim Diet". To complete the diet satisfactorily, the client has to eat all the recommended meals and not miss or substitute the recommended menu.

Techniques other than, or in addition to, dieting can be employed to help the client eat less. For example, he can be encouraged to serve his meals in smaller bowls and plates. He can then help himself to a serving which entirely covers the plate. The idea is that psychologically, the client's 'brain' perceives a 'full' plate as more satiating than a 'half full' one, even though the amount of food in the former may be less. Clients can also be advised to eat unhurriedly and to take their time savouring and chewing the food. Many clients admit when asked that they 'gobble' their food and never savour it. Other techniques have also been used to help a client control any pangs of hunger. Kroger (1977) suggests that the client can be taught to deal with any uncomfortable, hunger contractions by teaching the client to use glove anaesthesia. In this case, the client is trained under hypnosis to induce anaesthesia in his right hand. If he can do this during auto-hypnosis, he can then place his hand on his abdomen and 'transfer' the anaesthetised effect from his hand to his abdomen thus eliminating the hunger contractions in his stomach. I usually see clients over a period of two to four weeks i.e. four to eight sessions, depending on how they are coping with the diet and whether they are losing weight and how much. I never ask them to weigh themselves every day as this sometimes is very anxiety-producing and very often counter-productive for if a client has not lost weight on a particular day, he could lose his motivation. I therefore, recommend that clients weigh themselves undressed and on the same scales, positioned in the same place on the floor, before breakfast on the morning of the day they are due to see me or perhaps midweek and then again that morning. I sometimes also encourage them to keep a note of their feelings over the week particularly if they have had a moment of weakness and as one client once said "sinning". These "pecadillos" should not go unchallenged and should be discussed in the least punitive but firmest way possible.

Having decided on the course of action and agreed on the diet to be followed, the client is given specific, written instructions and menus (menus on their own are not comprehensive enough and do not, for example, give the client guidance on what, if anything, he can ingest between meals). It is a good idea for the client to purchase the book where the diet is explained fully, and if necessary major points can be discussed. Hypnotherapy comprises mainly appropriate post-hypnotic suggestion and ego strengthening related to the particular dietary needs, particularly how to deal with in-between meals nibbling and drinking. Specific reference can be made to the client under hypnosis about the food that has to be avoided and through ego strengthening suggest that the client does not need those foods and that he will be able to do without them quite comfortably.

I usually do not employ aversive-type suggestions but have done so on occasions with great success with certain clients when other more positive techniques have not succeeded (See Case Study 2, below). If the client's desired weight target is reasonable (and safe) and once his motivation for reducing weight is known, these two factors can be built into the hypnotherapy programme.

*Case Study 2*

Dassie was in her middle thirties, was 5 foot 7 inches tall and weighed 12 stones. She aimed to reduce to 10 stones over a period of time (which she subsequently achieved in two months). She was worried from the beginning that her partiality to sweets, chocolates, potatoes, bread and butter were going to be her downfall. She admitted to keeping a box of mint chocolates in the fridge and every time she opened the fridge she would help herself to a few pieces. She was also very fond of crisps and could go through several packets in one day.

Under hypnosis she was asked to imagine she was back at home and that she was standing in front of her fridge ready to open it to help herself to chocolates. She was encouraged to imagine that she was reaching for the box, and taking a piece of chocolate, and as she put it in her mouth she could experience a strange and disgusting taste as if the chocolates had gone off. It was suggested to her that she would therefore throw the whole box away. She was told that when she returned home after this session, she would in fact go for a piece of chocolate but she would not be able to eat it because it would taste foul. In order to reinforce this reaction, a further post-hypnotic suggestion was made that when she woke up she would yearn for a crisp which I would offer her from a sealed, fresh packet. However, the crisp would taste rancid and she would not be able to finish it.

When she woke up, though very aware of what I had suggested, she agreed to taste a crisp. Her reaction was such when she tasted it that she had to spit it out into her hand and insisted that the packet must be out of date. When shown that it was not, she could not believe it. At the next session, she confessed that the first thing she had done when she returned home was to go for the chocolates in the fridge. However, she took one look at the box and to her surprise felt no desire to take one. Dassie was taught auto-hypnosis which she practised very successfully. This client in fact did very well. Her motivation was that she had a generous wardrobe of very expensive clothes which she had outgrown and was looking forward to fitting into once again. We of course made use of this motivating factor and under hypnosis asked her to imagine trying those clothes on at her present weight. She complained that 'they did not fit'. A suggestion was next given that she should imagine herself as slim as she needed to be to get into one of her most expensive dresses and to then try it on. As she imagined herself doing this, a smile of gratification soon appeared on her face. She was thus, encouraged to 'think thin', particularly whenever she was tempted to break her diet in any way. She also felt that her husband would prefer her slimmer, an impression hotly refuted by him who said he fancied her any way she was! Two years after our first contact, she phoned me to say that she had put on four pounds since achieving ten stones and she was starting to crave for potatoes, cakes and puddings again. It took only a short hypnotherapy session to help her get rid of the craving. Some time later she contacted me again with a similar complaint which was dealt with successfully in the same way. Dassie was wise enough to ask for help when she noted the warning signs but many others do not. This is why monitoring progress over a period of time can be very productive.

As in most hypnotherapy programmes, clients should be trained in auto-hypnosis and encouraged to practise it as appropriate, particularly when they feel they are weakening. During the training, the hypnotherapist should provide for the client ego-strengthening strategies and 'verbalisation' which he can employ during auto-hypnosis, such as how good it would be to feel and be slimmer, and all the advantages of losing weight. The aim is to continuously help the client in his resolve not to relapse into bad eating habits even after the prescribed diet is terminated.

Sometimes, even though the client has requested hypnotherapy for reducing weight, he might not co-operate because of a conflict of interests whereby losing weight may imply an undesired consequence.

*Case Study 3*

Anne-Marie was an attractive professional lady who married in her middle thirties and whose husband's business kept him away from home five days a week.

In the first week, she lost five pounds but she admitted it was not as a result of following the agreed diet but because not having done so, she had almost fasted for two days so as not to fail in her objective. She was advised about the possible dangers of this practice and she promised not to repeat it. By the end of the second week she had acquired a nett weight loss of two pounds. The therapy was clearly not working and she agreed to discuss possible reasons for this. It in fact took her a little while to reveal the true reason. On the one hand she felt fat and horrible and knew she should diet. But she was terrified that if she did lose weight and regain her self-esteem, it would be much easier to respond to the advances she often received from male colleagues at work and possibly be unfaithful to her husband, thus jeopardising an otherwise happy marriage. We both agreed that whilst she continued to have this fear, it was perhaps better to postpone therapy until a more favourable time.

Some clients feel that they can not tolerate the behavioural symptoms which sometimes accompanies dieting, such as increased nervousness and intolerance of the smallest aggravation. Mothers with little children probably find it the hardest because their children are not always able to understand why mother has become so impatient with them. Such clients therefore, need help and encouragement during this period of time and perhaps the hypnotherapist should give more emphasis to these difficulties during ego-strengthening routines.

There are other reasons why hypnosis may not help an overweight client. One of them can perhaps be best explained through Kelly's theory of Personal

Constructs (Kelly, 1955; Bannister and Fransella, 1971). Particularly if the client has been overweight for a long time, he may find when he loses weight that he can not construe himself as a slimmer person and therefore finds himself in a role which is completely foreign to him. The uncertainties thus facing him as a slim person become too much and he then returns to becoming the 'previous person' and recovering the role he knows best, as an overweight individual. Other reasons for 'failure' may relate to the possible implications of losing weight such as other parts of the client's body becoming undesirably more prominent, or the inability to deal with certain stresses and pressures without resorting to eating to reduce them. Hypnotherapy, through relaxation and ego-strengthening techniques can help clients to become aware of such stresses and their consequences so that a client can rationalise his behaviour and be better able to deal with it. Hypnotherapy can help the client to confront anxieties in a more productive way. I have learned over the years that many clients who have come to me 'just to lose some weight' lead very stressful lives and very early on in the first session I ask them whether they savour their food or 'gobble it down'. The latter response almost invariably indicates that eating is anxiety related.

Some clients who do a lot of entertaining, particularly businessmen, do find it difficult to keep to a diet as they feel they might offend their guest or customer if they do not eat the same meal. Post-hypnotic suggestions can be given to these clients that they do not need to give in to these 'demands' for eating and drinking and that they can entertain just as effectively by ordering foods which are high in protein and low in fats, etc..

'Overeating' and 'undereating' e.g. as in bulimia and anorexia respectively, (See Chapter 4) may in fact be similar problems. Not uncommonly, both of these problems can be caused by more serious affective disorders such as depression. It is important to try and establish whether this is the case either from the client or his doctor, and unless the health care hypnotherapist is working in close collaboration with appropriate medical supervision, these cases should not be seen for hypnotherapy by those not appropriately qualified.

## Nailbiting and nail picking

This behaviour often underlies a state of tension or anxiety. When this relationship is confirmed, hypnotherapy can help the client to recognise these states and what causes them. Through counselling, relaxation, ego-strengthening and post-hypnotic techniques, he can be helped to reduce his tension and to deal with stress conditions in a more acceptable way. However, hypnotherapy may not be effective enough on its own and other strategies may have to be employed simultaneously. With young children, a 'token-economy' type of approach, together with hypnotherapy, might be helpful.

### Case Study 4

Jamie was a cheerful, gregarious and popular eleven year old. His nailpicking caused his parents tremendous concern as he often made his fingers bleed. The behaviour was not limited to his hand nails and when he could pick no more, he 'attacked' his toe nails. By and large he seemed like a well-balanced chap with some of the common school anxieties which did not appear to be unduly held. His father was a charismatic figure who himself cut his hand nails very short and on occasions would bite any edges off, though he maintained that his nail biting was confined to removing rough edges only. To what extent Jamie unknowingly bit his nails as a way of identifying with the very strong role-model his father presented was never established.

He achieved a trance in the first two sessions. On the third, he pretended he was in a trance and when asked to try and recall when he first started picking his nails, he said it went back to when his sister was born. In order to check how serious he was, I asked him to tell me how old he had been then. A quick check revealed that he had 'guessed' wrongly, not necessarily an uncommon phenomenon even in a subject in a hypnotic trance who is asked to 'recall' (as opposed to 'relive') an experience or memory. However, other signs led me to suspect that he was not in a trance. I 'woke' him up and challenged him about his having been in a trance state. After a few weak assertions, he agreed he had been acting. His father who was in the room asked him why he had laid the blame at his sister's door. Jamie protested that his sister got all the attention and proceeded to outline a catalogue of events which substantiated his claim. His father quoted yet other events as a counterclaim that Jamie had a fair share of the attention and benefits. This was an interesting confrontation since, knowing his father and following Jamie's acknowledgement of his father's claim, I could well believe that Jamie did in fact do quite well out of his parents. The fact though, was that Jamie did not see it as such. Again, to what extent this caused or contributed to his nail picking was not easy to establish.

At this point, it also became clear that hypnotherapy on its own was not likely to be effective. We therefore 'contracted' that we would use a token system and that when he reached a prescribed target, he could exchange his tokens for a desired object. His parents would examine his nails every day and if there was no evidence of picking, he would be given a 'star' which he would stick on a personal chart and bring to me at every session. In addition, I would award him a bonus depending on how well he had done over the whole week. He would also receive a penalty comprising a loss of stars, if he did not achieve certain goals. His final reward would be a very expensive leather jacket his father agreed to buy him if he did well.

A hypnotherapy programme was continued and Jamie seemed to thrive. After six weekly sessions, his nails were beginning to show white edges and several of them had grown just beyond his finger tips. Following termination of therapy, I monitored his progress every week. However, about a month later, his parents reported that though his hand nails were relatively intact, he was attacking his toe nails.

A further short course was unfortunately not productive; Jamie had somehow lost his motivation to the extent that depriving him of his coveted leather jacket did not seem to bother him. He was also not co-operating in entering hypnosis and no amount of discussion seemed to make any impact. Regrettably, one had to acknowledge that hypnotherapy might have had an ephemeral benefit but was not longer indicated. Ideally, one should have used some analytic technique to establish the reasons for his nail picking.

However, it seemed at the time that Jamie was no longer going to cooperate with such strategies and was beginning to somewhat resent missing out on other activities to come to the sessions.

## Conclusions

There are many other conditions which may respond well to hypnosis. In this book which is aimed at the health care professional, we have limited ourselves to discussing those which we are most likely to meet in the course of our work and which often are part and parcel of other conditions referred to us.

It is not inappropriate to reiterate that no one is entitled to agree to give hypnotherapy for conditions which are clearly outside their professional remit and expertise but this does not mean that we can not practise hypnotherapy for these conditions with a physician's or psychiatrist's approval, guidance and collaboration. It must also be stressed that in most cases, hypnotherapy is most effective when used as an adjunct to the more conventional therapy.

# Bibliography

**Abudarham, S. and Hughes, M.J.W.** (1983) 'Alternative Medicine - Has it a Role in the Remediation of Communication Disorders?', *Bulletin*, April, No 372. College of Speech Therapists.

**Adler, G.** (1966) *Studies in Analytic Psychology*. New York: Putnam.

**Bannister, D. and Fransella, F.** (1971) *Inquiring Man –The Theory of Personal Constructs*. Harmondsworth: Middlesex. Penguin Books.

**Barber, T. X.** (1965) 'Measuring "hypnotic-like" suggestibility with and without "hypnotic induction"; psychometric properties, norms and variables influencing responses to the Barber Suggestibility Scale (BSS)', *Psychological Reports*, 16, 809-44.

**Barber, T. X.** (1969) *Hypnosis: A Scientific Approach*. New York: Van Nostrand-Reinhold Co.

**Basker, M.A., Anderson, J.A.D. and Dalton, R.** (1975) 'Migraine and hypnotherapy', *International Journal of Clinical and Experimental Hypnosis*, 23, 1, 48.

**Bernheim, H.** (1886) *De la Suggestion et de ses Therapeutique*. Paris: Doin.

**British Medical Association** (1955) 'Hypnotism', *British Medical Journal*, 1, 1019.

**British Medical Association**, (1986) *Alternative Therapies*.

**Broussard, E.R.** (1976) 'Neonatal predictions and outcome at 10/11 years', *Child Psychiatry and Human Development*, 7, (2), 85-93.

**Brown, W.A and Heninger, G.** (1976) 'Stressed induced hormone release - psychologic and physiologic correlates', *Psychosomatic Medicine*, 38, 145-147.

**Christie, B. and Phillips, K.R.** (1988) 'Hypnosis in Occupational Psychology'. In: **Heap, M.** (Ed.) *Hypnosis – Current Clinical, Experimental and Forensic Practices*. London: Croom Helm.

**Cobb, S., Kasl, S.V., Roth, T.L. and Brooks, G.W.** (1974) 'Urinary norepinephrine in men whose jobs are abolished', *Psychosomatic Medicine*, 36.

**Deabler, H.L.** (1973) 'The use of hypnosis in lowering hypertension', *American Journal of Clinical Hypnosis*, 16, 2, 75.

**Dunnet, C.P and Williams, J.E.** (1988) 'Hypnosis in Speech Therapy'. In: **Heap, M.** (Ed.) *Hypnosis - Current Clinical, Experimental and Forensic Practices*. London: Croom Helm.

**Eisenberg, L.** (1977) 'Development as a unifying concept in psychiatry', *British Journal of Psychiatry*, 131, 225-37.

**Elman, D.** (1964) *Hypnotherapy.* Westwood: Glendale. CA.

**Erickson, M.H. and Rossi, E.L.** (1980) 'The Indirect Form of Suggestion'. In: **Rossi, E.L.** (Ed.) *The Collected Papers of Milton H. Erickson on Hypnosis,* Vol. 1: *The Nature of Hypnosis and Suggestions.* New York: Irvington Press.

**Evans, F.J.** (1972) 'Hypnosis and Sleep: Techniques for exploring cognitive activity during sleep'. In: **Fromm, E. and Shor, E.D.** (Eds.) *Hypnosis: Research Developments and Perspectives.* New York: Aldine Atherton.

**Ewing, E.** (1985) 'Hypnotherapy - A suitable case for treatment?', *Bulletin,* April, No 396, College of Speech Therapist.

**Eysenck, H.J.** (1943) 'Suggestibility and hysteria', *Journal of Neurology, Neuro-Surgery and Psychiatry,* 6, 22-31.

**Eysenck, H.J. and Furneaux, W.D.** (1945) 'Primary and secondary suggestibility', *Journal of Experimental Psychology,* 25, 485-503.

**Fellows, B.** (1988) 'The Use of Hypnotic Susceptibility Scales'. In: **Heap, M.** (Ed.) *Hypnosis - Current Clinical, Experimental and Forensic Practices.* London: Croom Helm.

**Forel, A.** (1956) *The Index of Psychoanalytic Writings.* Vol. 1

**Frankel, F.H. and Misch, R.C.** (1973) 'Hypnosis in a case of longstanding psoriasis in a person with character problems', *International Journal of Clinical and Experimental Hypnosis,* 21, 121.

**Fricton, J.P. and Roth, P.** (1985) 'The effects of direct and indirect hypnotic suggestions for analgesia in high and low susceptibility subjects', *American Journal of Clinical Hypnosis,* 27, 226-31.

**Gibson, H.B.** (1977) *Hypnosis - Its nature and therapeutic uses.* London: Peter Owen Ltd.

**Gruzelier, J.** (1988) 'The Neuropsychology of Hypnosis'. In: **Heap, M.** (Ed.) *Hypnosis – Current Clinical, Experimental and Forensic Practices.* London: Croom Helm Ltd.

**Hamson, L.** (1974) *Report to the British Society of Medical and Dental Hypnosis.* London.

**Hart, B.** (1985) 'Type of suggestion and hypnotisability in clinical work', *British Journal of Experimental and Clinical Hypnosis,* 2, 89-93.

**Hart, B.** (1988) 'Application to Psychological Therapies - Overview'. In: **Heap, M.** (Ed.) *Hypnosis - Current Clinical, Experimental and Forensic Practices.* London: Croom Helm Ltd.

**Hartland, J.** (1971) *Medical and Dental Hypnosis* (2nd Edn.) Baltimore: Williams & Wilkins.

**Heap, M.** (Ed.) (1988) *Hypnosis - Current Clinical, Experimental and Forensic Practices.* London: Croom Helm Ltd.

**Hilgard, E.R.** (1973) 'Dissociation Revisited'. In: **Hirle, M.** et al (Eds.) *Historical Conceptions of Psychology.* New York: Springer.

**Hilgard, E.R.**(1974) 'Towards a neo-dissociation theory: multiple cognitive controls in human functions', *Perspective in Biological Medicine*, 17, 301-16.

**Hilgard, E.R. and Hilgard, J.R.** (1983) *Hypnosis in the Relief of Pain*. California, Los Angeles: W. Kaufman Inc.

**Hilgard, J.R.** (1970) *Personality and Hypnosis*. Chicago: University of Chicago Press.

**Hill, O.** (1976) *Modern Trends: Psychosomatic Medicine*. London: Butterworths.

**Hinkle, L.E.** (1961) 'Ecological observations of the relationship of physical illness, mental illness and social environment', *Psychosomatic Medicine*, 23, 289.

**Hughes, M. J.W.** (1979) *An Evaluation of the Relationship between Life Events and Consultation Patters in General Practice*. PhD Dissertation, University of Birmingham.

**Hughes, M. J.W.** (1984) 'Psychological interactions in cancer', *Proceedings of the IMLS Cellular Pathology Group*.

**Hughes, M. J.W.**(1985) 'Psychological interactions among patients with ovarian cancer - psycho-immune and endocrine variables', *Proceedings of the IMLS Cellular Pathology Groups*.

**Hull, C.L.** (1933) *Hypnosis and Suggestibility*. New York: Apple Century-Crofts.

**Janet, P.** (1925) *Psychological Healing: A Historial and Clinical Study*. New York: Macmillan.

**Keele, C.A. and Neil, E.** (1978) *Samson Wright's Applied Physiology*. UK, Oxford: Oxford University Press.

**Kelly, G.A.** (1955) *The Psychology of Personal Constructs*. Norton.

**Khansari, D.N., Murgo, A.J. and Faith, R.E.** (1990) 'Effects of stress on the immune system', *Immunology Today*, 11, 5, 170-75.

**Kroger, W.S.** (1977) *Clinical and Experimental Hypnosis*. Philadelphia: J.B. Lippincott Co.

**Laquarte, J.K.** (1976) 'The use of hypnosis with children with deviant voices', *International Journal of Clinical and Experimental Hypnosis*, 24, 98-104.

**Latimer, P.** (1979) 'Psychophysiological disorders: A critical appraisal of concept theory illustrated with reference to irritable bowel syndrome', *Psychol. Med.*, 9, 1, 71-80.

**Ley, P.** (1979) 'Memory for medical information', *British Journal of Social and Clinical Psychology*, 18, 245-55.

**Lockhart, M.S. and Robertson, A.W.** (1977) 'Hypnosis and speech therapy as a combined therapeutic approach to the problem of stammering – A study of thirty patients', *British Journal of Disorders of Communication,* 12, 2.

**London, P.** (1965) 'Developmental experiments in hypnosis', *Journal of Projective Techniques and Personality Assessment,* 29, 189-99.

**Luchsinger, R. and Arnold, G.E.** (1965) *Voice, Speech and Language.* Wandsworth Publishing Co.

**Maher-Loughman, G.P.** (1970) 'Hypnosis and autohypnosis for the treatment of asthma', *International Journal of Clinical and Experimental Hypnosis,* 18, 1.

**Maher-Loughman, G.P.** (1976) 'Hypno-autohypnosis in Treating Psychosomatic Illness', In: **Hill, O.** (Ed.) *Modern Trends in Psychosomatic Illness.* London: Butterworths. p.440.

**Maher-Loughman, G.P., McDonald, N., Masona, A. and Fry, L.** (1962) 'Controlled trial of hypnosis in the symptomatic treatment of asthma', *British Medical Journal,* 2, 371.

**Marcuse, F.L.** (1982) *Hypnosis – Fact and Fiction.* Harmondsworth, Middlesex: Penguin Books Ltd.

**Martin, P.** (1987) 'Psychology and the immune system', *New Scientist,* 191, 435.

**Mason, C.F.** (1961) 'Hypnotic motivation in aphasics', *International Journal of Clinical and Experimental Hypnosis,* 9, 297-301.

**May, S.R.** et al (1983) 'Effects of early hypnosis on the cardiovascular and renal physiology of burn patients', *Burns Incl. Therm. Journal,* 9, (4) 257-66.

**McCue, P.A.** (1988) 'Milton H. Erickson: A Critical Perspective'. In: **Heap, M.** (Ed.) *Hypnosis – Current Clinical, Experimental and Forensic Practices.* London: Croom Helm Ltd.

**Meares, A.** (1960) *A System of Medical Hypnosis.* London: Saunders.

**Mellett, P.G.** (1973) 'Emotional aspects of asthma', *Health,* 10, 39.

**Melzack, R. and Torgerson, W.S.** (1971) 'On the language of pain', *Anaesthisiology,* 34, 1, 50-9.

**Meyer, E.K.** (1989) 'Changes in regional cortical blood flow in hypnosis', *Journal of Psychosomatic Medicine and Psychological Analysis,* 35, (1), 16-19.

**Moon, T. and Moon, H.** (1984) 'Hypnosis and childbirth: Self report and comment', *British Journal of Experimental and Clinical Hypnosis,* 1, 49-52.

**Moore, I.E.** et al (1983) 'Hypnotically accelerated burn wound healing', *American Journal of Clinical Hypnosis,* 26, (1), 16-19.

**Moore, N.** (1965) 'Behaviour therapy in bronchial asthma', *Journal of Psychosomatic Research,* 9, 257.

**Morgan, A.H. and Hilgard, J.R.** (1978-79) 'The Stanford Hypnotic Clinical Scales for Adults', *American Journal of Clinical Hypnosis,* 21, 134-47.

**Orne, M.T.** (1962) 'Hypnotically Induced Hallucinations', In: **West, L.J.** (Ed.) *Hallucinations.* New York: Grunne and Stratton.

**Pavlov, I.** (1923) 'The identity of inhibition with sleep and hypnosis', *Scientific Monthly,* 17, 603-608.

**Rissman, R.** (1987) *Family Systems Medicine,* 5, 4, 447-65.

**Richter, P.** (1928) *Das Stottern und Seine Heilung Durch Hypnotische Suggestion (Stuttering and its Healing through Hypnotic Suggestion).* Dresden: Rudolph.

**Rousey, C.L.** (1961) 'Hypnosis in speech pathology and audiology', *Journal of Speech and Hearing Disorders,* 26, 258-262.

**Rowley, D. T.** (1986) *Hypnosis and Hypnotherapy.* Beckenham, Kent: Croom Helm Ltd.

**Sacerdote, P.** (1982) 'Techniques of Hypnotic Intervention with Pain Patients'. In: **Barber, J. and Adrian, C.** (Eds.) *Psychological Approaches to the Management of Pain.* New York: Brunner Mazel.

**Sarbin, T.R. and Coe, W.C.** (1972) *Hypnosis: A Social Psychological Analysis of Influence Communication.* New York: Holt, Reinhart & Winston.

**Schleifer, S.J., Keller, S.E., Camerino, M., Thornton, J.C. and Stein, M.** (1983) 'Suppression of lymphocyte stimulation following bereavement', *Journal of the American Medical Association,* 250, 374-77.

**Schneck, J.M.** (1965) *Principles and Practice of Hypnoanalysis.* Springfield, Illinois: Charles C. Thomas.

**Shor, R.E. and Orne, E.C.** (1962) *Harvard Group Scale of Hypnotic Susceptibility (HGSHS).* California, Palo Alto: Consulting Psychologists Press.

**Solomon, G.F.** (1981) In: **Ader, R.** (Ed.) *Psychoneuroimmunology.* Academic Press.

**Spanos, N.P.** (1982) 'Hypnotic behaviour: A cognitive, social psychological perspective', *Research Communications in Psychology, Psychiatry and Behaviour,* 7, 199-213.

**Spiegel, H.** (1976) *Manual for Hypnotic Induction Profile (HIP): Eye-roll Levitation Method.* New York: Soni Medica.

**Stein, C.** (1963) 'The Clenched Fist Technique as a hypnotic procedure in clinical psychotherapy', *American Journal of Clinical Hypnosis,* 6, 113-19.

**Stein, M., Schiari, R.C. and Camerino, M.** (1976) 'Influence of brain and behaviour on the immune system', *Science,* 191, 435.

**Stratton, P.M.** (1977) 'Criteria for Assessing the Influence of Obstetric Circumstances on Later Development'. In: **Chard, T. and Richards, M.** (Eds.) *Benefit and Hazards of New Obstetrics*. London: Heinemann.

**Tarnower, H. and Sinclair Baker, S.** (1979) *The Complete Scarsdale Medical Diet*. London: Bantam Books.

**Theorell, T.** (1970) *Psychological Factors in Relation to the Onset of Myocardial Infarction and to Some Metabolic Variables*. Stockholm: Karolinska Institute.

**Udolf, R.** (1981) *Handbook of Hypnosis for Professionals*. New York: Van Nostrand Reinhold Co.

**Van Riper, C.** (1973) *The Treatment of Stuttering*. New Jersey, Englewood Cliffs: Prentice Hall, Inc.

**Vingoe, F.J.** (1968) 'The development of a group Alert-Trance Scale', *International Journal of Clinical and Experimental Hypnosis*, 16, 120-32.

**Wagstaff, G.F.** (1981) *Hypnosis, Compliance and Belief*. Brighton: The Harvester Press.

**Wagstaff, G.F.** (1988) Current Theoretical and Experimental Issues in Hypnosis: Overview. In: **Heap, M.** (Ed.) *Hypnosis – Current Clinical, Experimental and Forensic Practices*. London: Croom Helm Ltd.

**Waxman, D.** (1981) *Hypnosis – A guide for patients and practitioners*. London: Unwin Paperbacks.

**Waxman, D.** (1989) *Hartland's Medical and Dental Hypnosis*. (3rd. Edition). London: Balliere Tindall.

**Weitzenhoffer, A.M. and Hilgard, E.R.** (1959) *The Stanford Hypnotic Susceptibility Scales - Forms A and B (SHSS - A and B)*. Palo Alto, California: Consulting Psychologists Press.

**Weitzenhoffer, A.M. and Hilgard, E.R.** (1962) *The Stanford Hypnotic Susceptibility Scales - Form C (SHSS - C)*. Palo Alto, California: Consulting Psychologists Press.

**White, R.W.** (1941) 'A preface to the theory of hypnotism', *J. of Abnormal Psychology*, 36, 477-505.

**Wilson, D.K.** (1979) *Voice Problems of Children*. (2nd. Edition). The Williams and Williams Co.

**Wilson, C.S and Barber, T.X.** (1978) 'The Creative Imagination Scale (CIS) as a Measure of Hypnotic Responsiveness: Applications to Experimental and Clinical Hypnosis', *American Journal of Clinical Hypnosis*, 20, 235-49.

# Index

Abreaction 75
Alert Trance 18
Anaesthesia 116
– glove 115, 132
Analgesia 69-70 (See also Pain Relief)
Anxiety States (See Hypnotherapy)
Auto-hypnosis 67-70, 104-105

Case History Taking 37-38
Children 59-61
Client Preparation 40-41
Communication Disorders 97-108
– aphasia 102
– associated problems 107-108
– dysphonia 106, 107-108 (See also Voice)
– general considerations 98-99
– literature review 99-100
– neurological conditions 102
– stuttering 99, 101-102, 105, 106, 107
– voice/vocal problems 99-100, 102, 106
Confidence 103-104 (See also Hypnotherapy; Ego Strengthening)
Contra-indications 38-39, 88-89

Deepening Techniques 62-64
– arm levitation 62-63
– arm rigidity 63
– non-active visualisation 64
Diagnostic Scan (See Hypnoanalytic Techniques)

Ego Strengthening 64-66, 87, 103-104, 148
Ethical Considerations 61-62

Hyperventilation 57-58, 88
Hypnoanalysis 29-30, 85
Hypnoanalytic Techniques 70-75
– diagnostic scan 71-72

– hypnopictography 74
– identifying causal factors 86, 87, 102-103
– other techniques 74-75
– regression analysis 70-74, 87, 103
– structured dream analysis 74
Hypnosis
– (with) children 59-61
(See also Ethical Considerations)
– definitions 16
– historical overview 13-16
– hypnotic state (theories) 18-20
– reluctance to come out 58-59
– sleep v. hypnotic states 16-18
– symptom removal 83-85
– theories 18-22
Hypnotherapy 29-30, 80-82, 85
– analgesia 69-70 (See also Pain Relief)
– anxiety states 89-91
– asthma 91-92
– behaviour modification 105-107
– bulimia nervosa 95-96
– burns 122
– cancer pain 115-117
– confidence 118-119
– counselling 86
– depression 88, 89
– desensitisation 104
– general medical procedures 121-122
– insomnia 94-95
– migraine 92-93
– nail biting/picking 135-137
– pain relief 69-70, 81, 85, 112-113 (See also Analgesia)
– physical training 119
– physical trauma 110-111
– post operative pain 114-115
– post traumatic pain 117
– psychosomatic conditions 85-87
– psychotherapy 85, 86

Index 145

- rehabilitation 110-111
- relaxation 82-83
- road running !19-120
- skin problems 122-124
- smoking 108, 125-130
- sports training 119-121
- stuttering (See Communication Disorders)
- symptom removal 83-85
- voice problems (See Communication Disorders)
- weight loss 107-108, 130-135
- weight training 120

Hypnotisability 23-28
Hypnotic State Theories 18-20

Ideomotor Response (IMR) 56-57, 147
Induction Techniques 49-52, 59-61
- active 52, 60-61
- 'beachball' 60-61
- 'blackboard' 61
- combined 51-52
- deepening (See Deepening)
- Erickson's 'confusional' 50
- eye fixation 51, 146
- intermediate 50-51
- 'picture visualisation' (TV) 61
- relaxation 51, 52, 82-83

Interview 37-38

Miscellaneous Conditions 125-137 (See also Hypnotherapy)
Motivation 39-40

Nail Biting/Picking (See Hypnotherapy)
Neurolinguistic Programming (NLP) 49

Pain 112-117 (See Hypnotherapy)
- measurement of 112-113
- relief (See Hypnotherapy)
- thermometer 112-113
- threshold 112

Patient Selection and Preparation 35-47
Physical and Related Conditions 109-124

Post Hypnotic Suggestion 66-67
Psychologically Related Conditions 77-96
Psychosomatic Conditions 77-79, 80, 85-87
Psychosomat c Repertoire 80

Rehabilitation 110-111
- physical trauma 110
Relaxation 52, 82-83, 100 (See also Hypnotherapy and Induction Techniques)
Resistance 52-53
- overcoming 52-53

Self-hypnosis (See Auto-hypnosis)
Smoking (See Hypnotherapy)
Sports Training (See Hypnotherapy)
Susceptibility 23-28
- measurement of 29 (See also Susceptibility Tests)
Susceptibility Tests 41-46
- 'arm heaviness/levitation' 43-44
- 'body sway' 43
- 'hand clasp' 42
- 'orange' 42-43
- 'objective' 44
- 'postural sway' 43
Suggestibility 23-27
Suggestion 22-23
- nature of 22-23
- post hypnotic 66-67

Termination 75-76
Trance 53-56
- alert 18
- depth 28, 54-55
- evaluating depth 54-55
- evaluating speed 54-55
- signs 53-54
- speed 54-55
Triggers 56-57

Weight Loss (See Hypnotherapy)
Weight Training (See Hypnotherapy)

# Appendices

## Appendix A: 'Eye-Fixation' and 'Progressive Relaxation' Induction Routine

"With each breath you are taking now, so you are getting more relaxed and more tired, and as you are getting more relaxed and more tired with each breath you are taking, so, quite naturally, your eyes are getting tired, and as your eyes are getting more and more tired with each breath you are taking, so your eyelids are getting heavier and heavier, and as your eyelids are getting heavier and heavier with each breath you are taking so your eyes are closing, your body is relaxing, and you are drifting down, and down, into a deep relaxed state."

(Repeat this if necessary to obtain eye-closure).

Once the eyes are closed:-

"Yes, with each breath you are taking, so you are getting more relaxed and more tired, and as you are getting more relaxed and more tired with each breath you are taking, so all the muscles in your neck are relaxing more and more with each breath you are taking, so quite naturally, your head is feeling heavier and heavier. And as your head is feeling heavier and heavier with each breath you are taking, so your head is gently falling further and further to one side, into a comfortable, relaxed position. And as your head is falling further and further to one side with each breath you are taking, so this is helping you to go deeper and deeper into relaxation."

(Repeat if necessary)

Once the muscles in the neck have relaxed:-

"Already you are beginning to relax so very well, and because you are beginning to relax so well, with each breath you are taking now so you are going deeper and deeper into relaxation. And as you are going deeper and deeper into relaxation with each breath you are taking, so all the muscles in your body are relaxing more and more, in exactly the same way that the muscles in your neck relaxed a few seconds ago, and are continuing to relax. And as all the muscles in your body are relaxing more and more with each breath you are taking, so your body is feeling heavier and heavier. And as your body is feeling heavier and heavier with each breath you are taking, so you are going even deeper and deeper into relaxation."

(Repeat if necessary)

"Yes, you are really relaxing very well now, and in a few seconds time I shall be helping you to relax utterly and completely. In a few seconds time I shall say the word '**NOW**', and when I say the word '**NOW**', every muscle in your body is relaxing. Yes, even the very smallest muscles from the top of your head all the way down to the tips of your toes. Every last ounce of tension is going out of your body, and your body is sinking down completely and utterly limp. In fact your body is so limp it is actually feeling heavy, so heavy it is just as if your body is no longer a part of you. This is a pleasant feeling, and because it is pleasant, you are forgetting all about your body and going into the deepest most relaxed state you have ever, ever been in.

"So ready ... '**NOW**'. That's it. Let every muscle in your body relax. Let all the tension just ebb away. Good. And now let your body sink down completely and utterly limp. Just let your body become so limp that all your body is feeling heavy. You have got this relaxed heaviness in your head and neck, and *now* I want you to let that feeling of heaviness go all the way down through your body, to your finger-tips and down to the tips of your toes.

"Good. And now as your body continues getting heavier and heavier, as you are relaxing more and more, you are forgetting all about your body, and going into the deepest most relaxed state you have ever, ever been in. And with each breath you are taking so you are going deeper and deeper into relaxation.

"And I just want you to lie there now, breathing freely, easily, and naturally, going deeper and deeper into relaxation with each breath you are taking, until I tell you it is all over in a few minutes time ... "

## Appendix B: Ideo-Motor (I.M.R.) Finger-Signalling Response Routine

"Now, in a few moments time, we are going to establish a link with your unconscious mind in order that it may help us resolve this problem that you have been having.

"So, in a few moments time, I shall say the word '**NOW**' and when I say the word '**NOW**' in a few moments time, so your unconscious mind, that deep inner part of your memory will take control of the first finger of your right hand - that is the index finger - and as it takes control, so your first finger of your right hand will start to feel lighter. In fact, it will begin to feel so light, that without any conscious effort on your part, so the first finger of your right hand is starting to rise effortlessly from your lap.

"And so, when I say the word '**NOW**' in a few moments time, your unconscious mind will take control of the first finger of your right hand, and very gently yet effortlessly, when I say the word '**NOW**' so the first finger of your RIGHT hand will lift up, higher and higher with each breath that you take. And as it begins to lift up, so you are not having to help it lift up. Instead you are just allowing things to happen just as and when they are ready.

(Any part of the above can be repeated if it is thought necessary).

"So ready .... '**NOW**'. And now you can feel the first finger of your left hand feeling lighter and lighter, and it is lifting *higher* ..... and *higher* from where it is resting.

"That's good ..... now let it lift higher and higher, and as your first finger rises higher and higher, so you are feeling more and more relaxed. That's it."

Having obtained the Ideo-Motor Response, one continues as follows

"And now your unconscious mind is retaining control of that first finger, but in the meantime, allow it to sink down again with the other fingers until we need to draw upon it again. And as your first finger touches your lap again, so you will feel even more relaxed than before."

## Appendix C: Ego-Strengthening Routine

Apart from ego-strengthening suggestions, attention must be paid to factors such as rhythm, repetition, stressing certain word/phrases, interpolation of pauses. A typical routine, following induction and deepening could adopt this approach :-

"And now you have become *so* deeply relaxed ... your mind is *so* sensitive ... *so* receptive to what I have to say ... that everything I put into your mind ... will sink deep into your unconscious ... into the deepest recesses of your mind ... and will cause a lasting impression there ... such that *nothing* will eradicate those beneficial suggestions ... because of the good they will do you. Consequently, the things I put into your unconscious mind ... will begin to exert a *greater* influence over the way you *think* ... *feel* ... *behave* ... And because these beneficial things remain embedded in your unconscious ... after you have left here ... when you are no longer with me ... they will continue to influence your thoughts ... feelings ... well-being ... *just* as surely, as powerfully when you are back at home (work)" etc.

Here, one can suggest to the patient that he can expect changes to continue in his everyday life after the trance state is terminated.

"Everything I tell you is going to happen to you ... for your own good ... and will happen every day ... *just* as strongly ... as powerfully ... as surely as when you are with me in this room."

Suggested statements that can be put to the patient/client/subject during a typical ego-strengthening routine are listed below. These can be utilised or modified according to the nature of the problem or illness presented by the patient.

The patient may be told that he/she will feel:-

Physically stronger and fitter, alert, wide-awake, less depressed, less discouraged, less fatigued. Will become more interested in what they do, think less about themselves, no longer dwell on their own problems or difficulties. Their nerves will become stronger, steadier; they themselves will become calmer, more composed, less apprehensive, capable of thinking more clearly. In specific situations (probably related to the nature of problem), they will find themselves less tense and more relaxed, better able to cope etc. In general, they will enjoy greater confidence, feel a greater well-being, feel safer and secure and rely more on their own efforts.